101 Things I Hate About Your House

A Premier Designer Takes You on a Room-by-Room Tour to Transform Your Home from Faux Pas to Fabulous

JAMES SWAN
WITH CAROL BEGGY
ILLUSTRATIONS BY STANLEY A. MEYER

Health Communications, Inc.
Deerfield Beach, Florida

www.hcibooks.com

Library of Congress Cataloging-in-Publication Data

Swan, James, 1961–

  101 Things I Hate About Your House : A Premier Designer Takes You on a Room-by-Room Tour to Transform Your Home from Faux Pas to Fabulous / James Swan with Carol Beggy ; Illustrated by Stanley A. Meyer.

     pages cm.

  Includes index.

  ISBN-13: 978-0-7573-1567-1

  ISBN-10: 0-7573-1567-4

  ISBN-13: 978-0-7573-9181-1 (e-book)

  ISBN-10: 0-7573-9181-8 (e-book)

  1. House furnishings. 2. Interior decoration. 3. Hospitality. I. Beggy, Carol. II. Title. III. Title: One Hundred One Things I Hate About Your House. IV. Title: One Hundred and One Things I Hate About Your House.

  TX311.S93 2011

  747—dc22

                                                                                                2010045174

HCI, its logos, and marks are trademarks of Health Communications, Inc.

Publisher: Health Communications, Inc.
       3201 S.W. 15th Street
       Deerfield Beach, FL 33442–8190

Illustrations ©Stanley A. Meyer
Cover and interior design by Larissa Hise Henoch

Contents

Introduction

A DISCONCERTING LOOK, A GASP, or a simple catch in the throat were the common responses I received from my friends when they heard the title of this book: *101 Things I Hate About Your House.* Some people would nervously laugh and ask with trepidation, "Is my house in there?" or, more rarely, defensively say, "My house better not be in there," as if a gauntlet has been thrown down in preparation for a bloody duel. I usually pause, for effect, and reply as though searching for redemption from a particular decorating transgression, "No, not necessarily." My response is true enough, though admittedly vague; its ambiguity either masks a sustainable truth (what were they thinking with that shag sofa?) or conveys my mood, which most likely is dependent on the day of the week, the direction of the wind, or whether my new sweater makes my butt look big.

The act of creating is fueled by the total of life experience.

Someone once gave me this bit of wisdom: "The act of creating is fueled by the total of life experience." Truth, regardless of how we come to it, is just that—truth. So, in an indirect way, every room I've entered, looked at, dreamt of, or ran screaming from has influenced this book. Instead of gossipy storytelling or a "kiss and decorate" mentality, this book will provide you with my keen observations and bits of learning gleaned from years of study, practice, and mistakes I've made while pursuing the art of beautiful living. And lest anyone take this book, me, or themselves too seriously, please know that as much as I love the work that I do, I also understand that no lives will be saved by my fabric selections and no wars averted as a result of a deftly shaded lamp.

For me, it seems the writing was on the wall early in my life. As a child, I was told I had "champagne taste on a beer budget." This was confusing for me because I was neither interested in the cost of champagne nor beer; rather, I was very concerned about the poor furnishing choices I saw around me.

With one leisurely detour that included an undergraduate degree in theology and a minor in music, I made my way to the study of design and architecture and have created classically influenced interiors ever since. I have spent more than twenty years working for clients who have included captains of industry, movie studio heads, investment bankers, and real estate moguls. My work has put me on yachts and private jets, in luxury high-rise towers, and mountaintop retreats. I've done the great auction houses, been to the openings of the world's finest antique shows, and tromped through muddy barns on back country roads in far away countries—all in search of just the right piece. I've worked on homes built from scratch and on those expanding on an already beautiful idea. I've survived temperamental architects, contractors, craftsmen, and artisans (not to mention the occasional testy client) and live to tell the stories. I've made huge mistakes, had resounding successes, and tried to carry the battle scars of this wild and wonderful profession with a small degree of dignity and a big dose of humor. It is into this gaping void of the discretionary that I toss my insights knowing that whatever the balance in the bank, money spent to better our living environment is always discretionary. A home must respond to daily demands forced upon us by life, by the unbending laws of physics, and by any number of petulant voices in our heads. Practicality, while often unglamorous, is necessary when creating a beautiful home. "Tear down that bitch of a bearing wall and put a window where it ought to be" is the admonition barked by Faye Dunaway (playing Joan Crawford in *Mommie Dearest*) during a most memorable remodel, reminding us that if the basics

Beauty and grace evolve over time, like a good wine.

are not executed with consideration for our needs then "Houston, we have a problem."

I would like to state clearly the point of this book: my goal is to provide you with the basic principles you need to create a beautiful and gracious home. Beauty and grace evolve over time, like a good wine. A gracious home, while not always trumpeted in the glossy magazines, is one filled with collected objects of beauty comingled with the voices of friends, the laughter of family, and the relaxed acknowledgment of contentment. A gracious and beautiful home effortlessly considers the needs of its occupants and consistently rises to the occasion. We understand style and taste as being subjective, but principles for gracious living are not. While the former denotes mastery of historical nuance and devotion to a fickle public's fleeting fixations, the latter—and the object of our attention—is rooted in common sense piled high with practical experience.

The principles shared in this book will not cure cancer, usher in world peace, or get you into the size four jeans hanging in the back of your closet, but they will do one thing and do it consistently—the principles will work. I guarantee it. You don't have to be born with creative DNA or know how to mix stripes and patterns. You don't need to know how to spot the difference between Louis XIV and Louis XVI or have a clue who Baldwin, Draper, or Hampton are. Regardless of the state of your estate—be it massive or minuscule—or your Style IQ, these principles of gracious living will deliver a framework for a more beautiful and gracious home. Another way to look at this is that you can have fun with your home. I hereby give you permission to do so. If you can read, laugh, and jump start yourself into a modicum of action then you are well on your way to enjoying a more thoughtful, graceful, and beautiful home.

The title *101 Things I Hate About Your House* may prompt you to ask, what of all this talk of "hate"? As is often the case in literature, entertainment, and it seems, even politics—exaggeration is used to make a point. Diluting their content and potential for impact, too often design and decoration tomes read lightly in the area of critical comment fearing readers will take offense. Personally, I'd rather my good friends tell me I look frightful in my new blazer with its horizontal stripes rather than tacitly standing by while I make a fool of myself. When it comes to your home and all things pertaining to a gracious and beautiful way of life, you can count on me to call things as I see them. So yes, there are things about the American home that I can't stand. Believing, as I do, that love is closer to hate than indifference, I feel confident that anyone reading this book cares enough about their home not to mind the unvarnished truth.

> *Love is closer to hate than indifference.*

So, as not to miss a lick, we start at the street, move through the front door, and don't pause until we've taken a peek into every room of your house. I've also numbered the "101 Things" that make up this little volume so you can easily reference items you find helpful, painful, or just too funny to forget. I know of no better way than this to banish the foibles and follies and make fabulous the faux pas littering the homes of America.

Rest assured, it doesn't matter if your casa is inspired by an English cottage, a French farmhouse, an Italian palazzo, or last month's *Design Within Reach* catalogue. It doesn't matter if you have lots of money to spend or very little. It doesn't matter if you're ready to knock walls down, or already have, or if you've hired a general contractor, put the kids to work in a seedy sweatshop, or believe this to be the right time to sponge paint everything in sight. What does matter is that you genuinely want to experience your home in a more beautiful way and are prepared to lift a finger or two to realize that goal.

So, Dear Maker of Homes, here it is, the *CliffsNotes* for a more beautiful home. Quibble if you must about your own personal style and artistic vision; or sit quietly by, knowing that you've single-handedly raised the bar for the stylishly impaired. It matters not. There is room for all. The plan is simple; laugh a bit, learn a bit; and, most important, come to love your home as you've never loved it before. Now that's beautiful.

1

Entry Way

You Had Me at Hello

WE LEARN FROM A YOUNG AGE that first impressions are the most lasting. What takes seconds to perceive can be seared into an impressionable psyche forever—never to be washed away or painted over. That image can be played, replayed, fast-forwarded, rewound, enlarged, touched up, airbrushed, and edited in all manner of creative ways, but the initial impression will always remain. Great fiction writers know this. The right opening in a novel can grab your head and heart and propel you through any number of pages that follow. Hollywood certainly understands the power of the opening scene. Whether it is Harrison Ford racing for his life through a distant jungle in *Raiders of the Lost Ark,* or an elegantly paced journey through lavishly decorated parlors of nineteenth-century New York City in the opening moments of Edith Wharton's *The Age of Innocence*; first impressions make lasting impressions.

You have about eight seconds to make a first impression. Because every second counts, pay attention to what your doorway says about you and your family. Be clear, direct, and accurate. You won't get a second chance.

So what impression does your home make during those important first nanoseconds? Does "sleek and sophisticated" quickly come to mind? How about "warm and inviting," "relaxed and casual," or, decorating gods forbid, "nuclear devastation"? Take my advice and make your home's first impression a positive one.

1 A Dreary Little Mess

Nothing screams "Dreary Little Mess" quite like a front door masquerading as last winter's snow tires. Does the word "maintenance" mean anything to anyone? All paint was new, once. So how does your specially mixed "Nantucket Dew" look today? Have the kids, the dogs, and Mother Nature taken their best shots and won? My not-so-subtle suggestions might read something like: Clean it up! Wipe it down! Patch it, paint it, stain it, wax it, but just get the door to your home speaking a civilized language that's perfectly synchronized with the impression you wish to make.

That is, unless white-trash-travesty is what you had in mind, and if that is the case just set the book down (preferably where someone else will find it and reap the rewards of its wisdom) and find a cliff suitable for jumping.

If cliff-jumping isn't your cup of tea, may I suggest any of the following, in no particular order:

- Dilute a quarter cup of Murphy Oil Soap to warm water in a small pail. Wear rubber gloves to protect your manicure and mix in a bit of elbow grease and you may not recognize your door of entry. Repeat twice a year.
- For the dings and chips, which Murphy can't help, find a helpful hardware store and avail yourself of the caulk, putty, and paint. Helpful attendants can steer you to the right product and guide you in its proper use. Just do it.
- If your entry door's stain has seen better seasons, it may be time to strip off the wax or clear coat and begin anew. For a list of products to speed you on your way, you can visit our website at www.101ThingsIHateAboutYourHouse.com.

2   BULBS THAT BLIND

Dear Home Improvement Honey, banish the brutal level of light emanating from the lanterns hanging near your front door. When did *Escape from Alcatraz* become the inspiration for the light levels outside our homes? What part of a prison yard do you find attractive? Dangerous and ugly, blazing bare bulbs emit enough light to force visitors to confess to any manner of crimes. I can't tell you

how many flower beds I've stumbled into while shielding my eyes from a painfully incandescent glare from too much and too strong outdoor lighting. Even more upsetting, I've gouged the leather on a pair of gorgeous Prada shoes when I misjudged a step while blinded by spotlights beckoning me along a walkway.

Consider a bit of etching or frosting on the glass of outdoor lanterns to reduce glare, or simply use 40-watt bulbs, and always purchase the frosted variety. Lower wattage bulbs may be used in wall-mounted or hanging exterior lanterns when alternate light sources are woven into the landscape around your home. Interesting new solar technologies as well as hyperefficient LED technology are popping up in lighting catalogs and garden centers. You are not illuminating the neighborhood, providing landing guidance for large aircraft, or testing the viability of night growth in suburban shrubbery. To learn more you can visit the My Favorite Products Resource Center at www.101ThingsIHateAboutYourHouse.com.

3 MISSING MATS

A simple and effective tool for greeting guests and making a great impression is right under your feet. A fresh, clean entry mat helps keep out dirt and says you pay attention to details. Raising the bar higher and exceeding your guests expectations can be fun, rewarding, and easy.

Make sure to have a fresh and clean welcome mat resting on the entry step so your more socially adept acquaintances will wipe their feet. Remember, the more dirt you keep out the less dirt that gets in. Also, with a mat at the door your guests are more likely to pause a moment or two while they wipe the mud off their shoes (you know, the mud from their Riverdance through the flowerbed caused by the blinding lights.) This gives them time to stare through the clear glass panels (see below) on the front door and watch you run around the house in your bra and panties, while you chase the dogs and children and comb out your hair.

In most climates, and for most homes, a cocoa mat (made from the natural fibers of the coconut husk) is the most durable, efficient, and cost-effective option. Pithy messages, greetings, and monograms are best left for catalog photo spreads; though a plain mat with a classic black boarder is always appropriate. Locations prone to extreme weather conditions may find slotted wood or figured metal mats appropriate during particularly inclement seasons but should be replaced with the more welcoming cocoa mat when the sun shines again. Rubber mats are best left at the office or factory floor. Correct sizing of an entry mat is predicated on the dimensions of your entry door. When in doubt, opt for a version slightly wider than the door, as this will appear less stingy to your arriving guests and should cast you in the best light possible.

4   BARE NAKED GLASS

A little privacy, please. I don't care what your contractor said: no one except the guy wandering the neighborhood in a trench coat will find merit in a clear-glass paneled entry door. If you have one, hire someone to etch or frost it. Alternatively, cover the glass with inexpensive, yet elegantly sheared fabric, hung on beautiful little brass rods and stretched across the otherwise painfully transparent-glass panels. You can buy chic fabric panels and rods at any big box store or design center. Whichever option you choose, you'll add a touch of class and privacy to your front door and keep your friends and neighbors from knowing any more family secrets than they do already.

5 A Mirror-Less Entry Hall

Once the door to your home is flung wide to welcome your nearest and dearest and they have scraped mud off their feet and allowed a moment or two for retinal healing to take place it's time for the real game of *The Hostess With the Mostest* to begin. The first thing I look for is a mirror. The cry, "My kingdom for a mirror" bounces around in my head as I scan the walls of the halls of entry (be it sizable or small) hoping for a little help. Wind, rain, or a treacherous seatbelt can put an end to even the best hair days. Is it too much to expect a simply framed, mercury coated, plate glass reflective panel artfully hung in a friendly way? You know, something that reminds the visitor "Before you walk into the crowd just around the corner you may want to fix that bird's nest of a 'do teetering on your forehead!" Or, the even more intimate suggestion that hints, "Although we love you dearly, we fear that children and the elderly will be spooked by those false eyelashes masquerading as earrings." A casual glance in a mirror (that tool of vanity we thank the warlords of dynastic China for) can either send you boldly into the social fray without a worry in the world or cause your fingers to speed-dial a hair and makeup rescue team from the nearest beauty emporium.

A well-placed mirror in the hall of entry has little to do with personal vanity and everything to do with a host's kindheartedness. Few things are as cruel as allowing an unwitting guest to march into the social soiree looking a disheveled mess. Good hosts ensure their guests have the most positive experience possible, and this begins by allowing them an opportunity to look their best.

6 Mirror, Mirror Everywhere

In the real world we understand that too much of anything can be problematic and cause ugliness such as hangovers, muffin-tops, and grotesquely altered facial features. It can be the same in your

entry hall. A simple mirror is one thing. Every surface covered in reflective glass is just too much. All I need is a glance to assess the overall damage. What I don't need is an endless repetition of my rumples, wrinkles, and wind-swept atrocities spun round me like the lame-clad cast of *A Chorus Line*. Remember, just a glance.

7 Down Lights of Death

And speaking of performances on the big stage, what's up with the stadium lighting inside the house? Does no one know the simple joys of "dimming?" It's modern magic, really, these little boxes with wires and toggles and dials and such that allow you to control the level of light put out by the three dozen mercury lamps you have strapped to the ceiling of your entry hall. Think candlelight, people! Ever wonder why everyone in Merchant-Ivory films looks so great? It's the candlelight. Keep light levels hovering close to a flicker and not only will you look amazing, but your guests will, too. When in doubt install dimmers on every light in the house; its the best protection for an overlighting tendency.

Think of the function of the room when considering lighting. When a room serves more than one purpose, dimmer switches come in handy so you can adjust the light level to your liking or need. Besides function, consider the ambience you desire. Lighting has a dramatic effect on how you feel.

8 SMELLING A RAT

Besides the "look" of a house, a host or hostess should consider another layer of impression with which to astonish and astound unwitting guests. Breathe with me. Take a deep breath and try not to choke on the aroma of musty wet dogs, acrid cat boxes, marinating gym clothes, and damp, moldy laundry. To put it succinctly: Buy a candle. I can walk into most convenience stores today and find something that resembles a scented candle. How difficult can it be to offer gentle scents to your guests as they enter your home? Think in terms of "pleasant and welcoming" if not downright "sexy and sophisticated." Why offer the dank smell of ordinary? Use your imagination. The aroma of baked cookies is better by far than that of Fido and Fifi in all their pungent-familial glory.

SCENTED SPLENDOR

If filling your casa with sublime scents seems a daunting dilemma, here's a list of options at which you won't turn up your nose:

POTPOURRI. A mixture of dried, naturally fragrant plant material is a simple addition to any home. Bought by the bag in a wide range of fragrances, this colorful household addition can be placed in wood or porcelain bowls throughout the house.

AROMA STICKS. Diffusers of scented oils are a fresh, modern alternative to potpourri or candles. Their graceful presentation is a lovely addition to any room in the house.

SCENTED CANDLES. Staples in elegant homes for decades, these glowing devices add elegant aromas and the magic of an open flame year round.

PLUG-INS. These electrically warmed delivery systems often utilize synthetic scents and should be avoided unless no other options are available.

Unless you wish your guests to feel dazed and confused, keep the scent for your home consistent from front door to back. The experience is seamless and much less prone to causing headaches than the hopscotch, scent-per-room approach attempted by the less well informed. If confusion reigns and you don't know which scent to choose, go to www.101ThingsIHateAboutYourHouse.com where you'll find listings of our favorite aromatic providers and our top-ten favorite scents of all time.

9 THE SOUND OF SILENCE

Lest we neglect one of our five senses and find ourselves lacking in sensibility, may I draw your attention, Dear Docent of the Doorway, to the screeching silence that hangs like finely crafted couture from the boney shoulders of runway models during fashion week. It's fine if you care to wallow in the bowels of a soundless fortress guarded from the sweet, sassy, and sexy sounds of life, love, and just music in general. But when other humans are involved—be they guests or family or even casual acquaintances—it's up to you to elevate the experience and lay out layers of sounds that entice and entrance or at least don't cause unease and discomfort. Music is that lovely invisible guest that can soothe the awkward moment and shrink the sting of silence when an interaction of any size seems to be slow to catch fire and burn with its own energy. Simple background music can save your hosting derriere and make people feel warm and perfectly at home no matter how socially inept one of your workmates may be.

With music, managing the question of volume is monumental for its success. Prior to the guest's arrival, the rooms of entertainment should be filled with its presence. As guests arrive the hosts' assumes the task of volume control, always allowing for easy conversation over a mellifluous background but never drowning out the tidbits of wisdom being batted about your living room. As for the choice of tunes, read the room and deliver music your guests will enjoy, appreciate, and can identify. Nothing will kill a party faster than genre inappropriate music. When in doubt create a playlist that you love; it is, after all, your home. If they're enjoying you, they'll doubtless appreciate your tunes.

10 A DISORGANIZED MESS

It can happen to the best of us. And the very best, like cream, continue to rise to the occasion and find snappy, sassy ways to deal with the clutter of life (old boyfriends, last season's fashion tomes, and ubiquitous coupon books from every pharmacy and dime store within a ten-mile radius). In this order consider: Any stand of trees on the nearest mountain for the old boyfriends; beautiful baskets or fabric covered storage boxes to house your growing collection of *Vogue, Elle, Decor,* and *The World of Interiors*; and the recycling bin for every coupon book and random catalog that comes through your mail slot. If they are important to you, use them. Don't store them on the entry hall table. Ever!

LOVE IT OR HATE IT, but here's a favorite entry hall from a client's home in Los Angeles. In this shot you only have a partial view. The hall table, mirror, and coat closet are out of frame; and yes, I ignored my own tip when we elected stone floors rather than an area rug. Carpet on the stairs counts! On your march toward a successful entry be sure to include a well-thought-out lighting plan. Put shades on your chandelier bulbs, sconces, and all table lamps. Line your shades with pale pink silk. Install dimmers on all ceiling cans, chandeliers, sconces, and lamps. Always install a framed mirror. Pick a signature scent that you love. A scented candle or potpourri is a must at the entry of every home. Select a signature scent that your guests will always recognize as your own. Develop a well-appointed guest closet. Designated space in a convenient closet makes guest coats and bags a snap to hide. Matching wooden hangers with lavender sachets make opening the closet a pleasure. Yes, find and buy a beautiful rug. The rich tones of a favorite area rug make a beautiful and lasting first impression. Whether an antique, Oriental, or new work of art, an area rug at your entry hall is always a good design investment.

2

Powder Room

Excuse Me While I Powder My Nose

INTO ANY HOUSE A GUEST MAY WANDER and at some point that guest will need to freshen up. If you live in a studio walk up in the East Village or a rambling colonial in the Midwest, you will need to give thought to where you will guide the guest who needs to—well, powder their nose! It may mean they are sharing the space you and your curling iron occupied moments ago or it may be a quaint suite of rooms off the entry hall where guests can powder, primp, and linger until they are ready to claw their way, through the loitering crowds, into your drawing room. So pick up a pad, take a few notes, and be the host your mother never thought you could be!

11 A LIGHTLY POWDERED DISASTER

The first step in getting the powder room right is to clean the place up. If I've got to "go" then the last thing I want to see is the collection of cover-sticks, deodorants, and hair products that went into pulling you together for either day, evening, or both. I love you dearly, but I don't love you that much. Put your stuff away. If you are strapped for space then think outside the box. If need be, sweep it all into a basket or plastic storage container and chuck it under the vanity or into a closet in your bedroom but don't, I repeat don't, make me stare at your collection of impulse buys from every beauty outlet in town.

12 Playing Hide-and-Seek

Life is all about balance, isn't it? So it is with your powder room. Put your things away? Yes. Hide everything from your guests? No. Not unless you want them using the shower curtain as a hand towel. The drill is simple, really. Stand outside your powder bath (or bathroom designated for guests) and let your mind wander. Let it wander so far away that you forget where you are. You've now become a stranger in your own home. Perfect. Take a tentative step across the threshold and I dare you to find your way through the potty process without your blood pressure elevating into the danger zone. Let's start with the paper products. Are there any? If yes, then are they stocked for company? (Less politely stated, are there more than three squares of paper on the roll?) Is there back-stock located in a reasonable, logical, and accessible location? Rolls artfully tossed in a basket on the floor, lovely. Backup rolls stacked

Consider every guest in your home a perfect stranger. Assume nothing while you strive to make their quiet moments of primping and powdering as stress free as possible. With my memory waning, I've created a powder room master list. This simple checklist itemizes the linens, papers, candles, soaps, lotions, perfumes, and various other ephemera that I believe belong at my guest's fingertips. Scanning the list I confirm everything in its place and I miss nothing!

neatly on a bracketed shelf, divine. On the point of these helpfully rolled squares of the softest of tissues, please orient the roll with the paper coming over the top toward those in need rather than dangling less than helpfully down the wall. Few things look as limp and forlorn as a tail of tissue evasively hugging the wall just out of sight. Please don't make your guests rummage through every drawer and cabinet in this and the adjoining rooms trying to find a fresh roll or a new box of tissues. And, Dear Purveyor of Practicum, don't be cute with the location of the waste basket. Next to the sink is fine. Tucked behind the water closet is reasonable, but spare your guests the hunt unless you want them to chuck their used tissue or finger towel behind the toilet for the next guest to discover.

13 LESS THAN HEAVENLY SCENTS

No matter how many times we've finished finishing school there are those awkward moments when our bodies do the stupidest things; shocking, indeed, but true. How very thoughtful of our host or hostess to salvage the remnants of our dignity by providing a scented spray or fragrant candle to help ease us back into the mix of polite society, so much more graceful for us than a roll of yellow police tape and instructions for sealing off the area until the EVAC team arrives. By placing sprays in prominent display on a featured table or stand you elevate their importance and encourage their use, eliminating any timidity on the part of your guests. When combined with a lit candle or aromatic oils, and maybe a small orchid or vase of cut flowers this display in your powdering room is both elegant and useful.

 ## 14   RUBBER-BACKED RUGS

As we've previously noted, balance is everything and with everything in balance tranquility reigns, peace echoes through the countryside, and lions and lambs snuggle. If *only*. Not every home has an independent powder room. Often a family bath does double duty serving the needs of the household as well as those of guests. Let's now consider the balance we seek when selecting a rug for our room for guests, whatever shape the room may take. Pay heed to the physical needs (cold floors), the aesthetic needs (color, pattern, pizzazz!), and the practical needs that are doubly concerning when or if the room is doing double duty.

Ready for a change? Want instant gratification? Craving a decorating fix? Immediately add color, pattern, and warmth to your powder room by adding a dazzling area rug. Types to consider: antique Orientals, ethnic flat weaves, plush Tibetans, rag rugs, and more.

Allow me to highlight two rug options available in every corner of the world. First, there is any rug with a rubber backing. Second, there is every other rug in the world. I understand the need that the dreaded rubber-backed "bath mat" yearns to address, that of a skidless experience, but I also have clear images of rapidly multiplying colonies of bacteria and fungus, not to mention the crumbling of rubber that has been tumbled dry one too many times and has become an unsightly mess. Just so we're clear: you have a world of options out there, why limit yourself to anything with a rubber backing.

With those lovely mental images firmly in place, shall we pivot and gaze longingly on the myriad other options available in the marketplace. The ranges of options are endless. The challenge is to change the way we think about these little rooms and their little rugs. As we realize the decorating opportunities offered in these wee little moments suddenly we can have some fun. Antique Oriental found at a tag sale for $25? Sold! Waffle-weave mat found at a chic European boutique? To which I say, do they take American Express? Hand-painted canvas drop cloth from an island-bound artist in the Mediterranean? Wrap it to go. Hook rug? Yes. Rag rug? Yep. Remember: Think outside the box. Make these little spaces sing with the unusual and the exciting. You have my permission. And yes, of course, for comfort and safely you should always install nonskid padding with any area rug in your home. Your guests will remain vertical and the life of your fabulous new treasure will be prolonged.

 ## 15 SOAP SOUP

Almost as bad as rubber-backed rugs and MIA guest towels, I venture to say that few things cause such indigestion (and on a perfectly empty stomach) as the sight of a wet, slimy, bubbly bar of soap. It matters not how lovely the brand or how delicious the dish in which this gurgling mass is fermenting. That bubbling glob of mush is unsightly; it's unsanitary (maybe not technically but somehow it's just icky) and (most dear to our hearts) it's just not beautiful. Let's take a stroll down retail alley. Pick a store.

Any store. From small chichi bou-
tiques to perfectly delightful mid-
size regional retailers to the big-boy
box stores, you can't swing a cat
without hitting a major display of
soap products. Loads of lavender.
Carts full of cardamom. Piles of
patchouli—you get the picture—
they are all lined up in the most
beautiful and useful gentle-action
pump containers just waiting to
squirt their way into your heart. High-
dollar brands come in beautiful bottles,
which can be deposited at your sink for imme-

*Upgrade your powder room
with this simple A-list trick;
nothing says luxury like a beautiful bottle of spa-style hand soap and
a small tray displaying its matching wrapped bar soap. You've just
elevated a mundane moment and
made it memorable. Don't stop now.
Look for other ways to make simple experiences more beautiful.
You're on your way to your
most gracious hosting
ever.*

diate use. Other mass-market brands and their generic
bottles are best left in the storage closet allowing you to select a
stylish and sophisticated dispensing bottle into which to pour the
former's contents. And, best of all, they come with coordinating
bar soaps, madly wrapped in the most delightful ways. This allows
you to display the wrapped bars because these are beautiful. It also
allows you to provide your guests with the sanitary and stylish use
of the liquid as they scrub the mud off whatever or wherever without having to pick up that nasty glob of scented slime. And, Dear
Guileless Guest, twenty lashes with a slimy, scented noodle should

you opt to strip bare one of those delicately wrapped bars when the liquid version is yours for the taking. If you ask me, your hostess should present you with a bill on your departure for such thoughtlessly rude behavior. Were you born in a barn?

High levels of light make rooms feel cold and unwelcoming. Don't let illumination get away from you. Stay in control of light levels in your home with dimmers. Some units simply plug into the wall giving you complete control over your table and floor lamps.

16 BLINDING LIGHT

There is not a room in the house that will not benefit from well-considered lighting. That said, there are few spaces in the home that will garner you, Dear Illuminator of All That Is Hospitable, the accolades reserved for triumphal Roman generals quite like the powder room. Consider for a moment the shock to the system when, after two or three too many of your notoriously chic agave and anisette cocktails, a guest stumbles to your powder room and flips the switch. Even the stout of heart will falter and sway when the blazing rays of a thousand suns scorch their liquor-laden eyes. More delicate creatures may simply be knocked to their knees and those of even greater fragility could, conceivably, spontaneously combust. What disaster that would be. How exactly do you share the news to an unwitting spouse, who also has not been shy about the libations, that the love of their life has been toasted by your powder room lighting? So, pray tell, what is one to do? Shocking in its simplicity, the solution is to remove every lightbulb higher than 60 watts. Immediately smash all clear bulbs under your well-shod foot and replace them with a kinder, gentler frosted species. Fixtures mounted on or recessed into the ceiling should never (in a powder room) be higher than 40 watts. If the fixture houses more than one bulb then reduce the wattage per bulb to 25. Sconces or counter lamps should contain 25-watt bulbs (frosted, please) and everything in the room should be on dimmers. The objective is to capture the essence of the soft, even, and understated illumination offered by candles. The glow emitted by these sticks of wax is positively sexy. Even your Aunt Gladys will glow with the dewy essence of youth not seen on her face since just after the Great Depression. I can assure you that after one trip to the powder room Aunt Gladys, not to mention your other guests, will perceive you to be a host of the Supreme Order. Make your guests look good (it really is all about the lighting) and you will, too.

17 AWOL HOSTESS TOWELS

Like a bull exhausted by all those damn red flags I wilt and whither when faced with questions about finger towels in a powder room.

When, if ever, do you pick up and use the exquisitely embroidered linen towels proudly displayed by conscientious hosts? The answer is simple; feel free to wreak havoc on any beautiful finger towel should your host neglect to provide you with the option of a paper guest towel. A well-appointed powder room will have heavyweight paper guest towels (often monogrammed) accessible at the sink (stacked in a small tray or basket) in addition to a lovely display of one-of-a-kind linen towels. The former are for use followed by disposal; the latter are intended to be decorative and appreciated as such. If no paper option exists then use the linen towel, refolding and rehanging it on your departure. Hosts, don't bitch about a collection of wadded up, wrinkled hand-embroidered linen guest towels if you don't offer guests a reasonable option on which to dry their hands. Find resources for beautiful paper guest towels as well as fine antique linens at www.101ThingsIHateAboutYourHouse.com.

18 A BOOKLESS REPOSE

Growing up, my grandmother displayed a cross-stitched masterpiece in her hall bath that sums things up rather nicely: "Who's that knocking at the door, one may never know. But tarry not my friend; he too may have to go." Smart and snappy might be the basket or Canterbury that holds magazines and pithy little volumes, but the larger question looms. Should a host encourage such a leisurely scan or should we support greater efficiency on our guest's part when they're powdering their nose, correcting their coiffure, adjusting what needs adjusting, and generally taking care of business? On this question, I long ago have made my choice and gladly admit I enjoy placing wee witty volumes, filled with interesting thoughts and pictures, in my powder room. I find that smartly edited books offer a unique opportunity for a host to bring a smile to the face of those who tarry for a while, or not. Fortunately, for those who really do have to go, I've got a second bathroom!

And remember when the books have been selected (avoid periodicals or your powder room will look like a doctor's waiting room) their display must be thoughtfully considered. Never on the back of the water closet—but always on a small table or stand. When considered as part of a larger tablescape, a stack of five or six books can be a charming, visual addition.

What to do with wet hands is a common dilemma for those using the powder room. As a good host, take the lead and eliminate any question in the mind of a guest. Display your heavyweight paper guest towels, on a tray or basket, conveniently at the sink. Allow your fine linen towels to be displayed on a less convenient hanging bar. Now that's beautiful!

HERE'S A POWDER ROOM created for a client that is beautifully appointed and elegant in the extreme. For a big decorating punch we upholstered the walls then detailed the upholstery with panels formed from applied tap trim. An antique chest was repurposed as a Pullman then fitted with a stone top and undermounted sink (when using stone always undermount the sink). A fabulous nineteenth-century Italian-carved gilt mirror was hung above the sink and the Pullman was detailed with a most beautiful collection of silver objet d'art. A dazzling antique Oriental prayer rug finishes out the room along with a unique collection of antique armorial engravings. While it may be a bit much for some tastes, this little room captures the essence of a well-appointed powder. Some don't ever want to leave!

3

Living Room

Go On, Live a Little

THE SERIOUS LACK OF LIVING occuring today in rooms intended for this purpose is fascinating. Whether through ignorance, arrogance, or the poor use of space planning, the room for living doesn't always meet the expectations of its name. Stale expanses of questionably constructed, overly decorated, infrequently occupied prime residential real estate hardly qualify as centers for elevated living. Rooms, both large and small, intended for life's special moments, sit quiet, empty, and thus lacking any tangible charm or beauty. Is there a wholesale cure for these living deficiencies? Only time will tell. In the meantime, we do what we can to bring life to the room of living.

Apartment dwellers dream of just one more room into which they may lead people or run from them depending on their relationship to the maddening crowd. Cocktails in the entry way followed by dinner at the kitchen island with desserts, coffee, and after-dinner cordials in the sitting/bedroom may be all a studio dweller has to offer. When offered with head held high and an eye toward making guests feel comfortable, even this diminutively scaled progression adds interest and charm to an evening. Imagine what you can accomplish with your split-level colonial or mid-century modern? Not using space within your home due to out-dated assumptions or prejudices is wasteful and should be avoided. If you're blessed with rooms for living then shame on you if you don't live in every single room.

19 Furniture Against the Wall

Who knew in 1973 that one little girl, a few gulps of split-pea soup, and furniture on wheels would cause such a ruckus? *The Exorcist* sent people screaming from theaters. People experienced extreme reactions to the movie, even losing their lunch during screenings; and I believe the horror resulted because of not only the green makeup, spinal contortions, and the voice of Satan but also because of the shocking, violent, and ugly reality of furniture

slammed up against the walls. The tiniest of spaces notwithstanding, most rooms for living will benefit greatly from pulling furniture away from the walls. Conversations become more natural, guests feel more at ease, and the entire experience of entertaining is enhanced when chairs, settees, and tables are arranged in ways that encourage intimacy.

A smaller-size sofa or settee grouped with two pull-up chairs, two lounge chairs with a small table tucked on the back side of an angled desk, or two slipper chairs facing each other at the fireplace—all move furniture off the wall and into the flow of great entertaining. Practice by moving your pieces around . . . there is no place to experiment and learn like your own living room!

20 TRAGIC HOUSE PLANTS

Unless you're ensconced in a sun-dappled solarium surrounded by your exotic collection of specimen orchids carted back from the

jungles of South America by your adventurous globe-trotting first husband who fell to his death while straining to secure a rare scented orchid, then I would give great pause to the inclination to bring the outdoors in. Invariably the beauty is lost in translation leaving your living room populated by scraggy, ill-potted, lifeless limbs screaming for the compost pile. Not to say that the desire to fill a lonely corner of your home with a stunning botanical specimen is an erroneous thought; but the rub, Dear Horticulturally Challenged Reader, falls into one, if not all, of the following three categories:

THE SCALE OF THINGS. Nothing gets swallowed by space with the same speed and consistency as do potted plants. That "tree" that seemed expansive when you shoehorned it into the back of your Mini Cooper suddenly looks like a twig-in-a-thimble when dropped next to a window or fireplace in your living room. Who knew? If you are determined to live in the jungle, apropos the set of *Apocalypse Now,* you will know you have the scale right when you need four strapping, sweaty deliverymen to haul the tree off a flatbed truck into your Casa del Botanico. Don't kid yourself. Size matters.

CONTAIN YOUR ENTHUSIASM.
So you've prevailed in the purchase of a mighty sequoia (or a merely

magnificent ficus) and as the contractors inch the John Deere tractor ever closer to your front door you realize, in a panic, that the burlap-wrapped root ball will cause disaster on your hardwood floors. With all your might please resist the inclination to pur- chase the ugly plastic tub. Much like a good shoe, a container can make or break the entire ensem- ble. Whether a chic little cachepot or a massive planter from the Musée de l'Orangerie near Versailles, always go for the most beautiful container (even if it is plastic) you can find. It does not have to be expensive, but it should certainly make you, like Lady Gaga, ready to "Just Dance."

TAKE CARE WHEN IT COMES TO CARE. As with many items around the house, proper maintenance enhances and extends the life and enjoyment of prized pos- sessions. Think of all the hard work you've put into your husband for goodness sake. Would you leave him parched for days on end, lacking proper cleaning and feeding? Would you allow his spindly branches to reach feebly upward without benefit of your caring and nurturing touch? Well, maybe so, but that's not the point. Plants need your care. They need it daily. They will die abruptly and pitifully, a haunting testimony to your less than mediocre attentions; and un- like your husband who can stumble around for quite a while without your doting and fretting, these little snippets of Mama Na- ture are toast without you. So don't scrimp. Care enough to hire the very best!

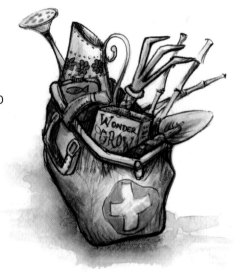

21 ABSENTEE TABLES

Say you're lucky enough to land a dinner reservation at that fabu- lous new restaurant everyone in town is clamoring to get into (you snagged the last reservation just before the Pittsburgh Pirates win the World Series again) and you get all dressed up and drive across town only to discover they don't have parking. I don't mean they just don't have valet. I mean no valet, no little lot-in-the-back, no homeless person offering to watch your car for ten bucks on the street in this up and coming neighborhood. I mean nothing. Zip. Zero. Zilch. Why it just takes all the Choo out of your Jimmys! It's

just not right. It's inconvenient. It's thoughtless and, well, you'll show them. You'll just never come back.

The point of this wee digression is that one should never inconvenience a guest. For instance, you should never force a guest to navigate through the minefield of chatter, platters, and libations, also known as your living room, only to alight on your smartly upholstered (in the French manner) eighteenth-century canapé and realize the only surface available to balance the Flora Danica plate, so generously offered by your catering staff, and the Baccarat highball glass filled to the brim with Jack and Coke—is one's own lap.

It's a simple test. Wander randomly through your home. Spontaneously sit and reach. If all you find beneath your sweaty palm is the air that we breathe then get thee to a shop, gallery, flea market, or tag sale and fill the void with a smart, stylish table of sorts.

22 A HORRIBLY EMPTY HEARTH

For those fortunate enough to possess a fireplace in their living room (or any room for that matter) a few thoughts on making the most of this gift from the decorating gods. Few elements in our modern home draw attention and anchor us to memories (real or imposed by Hollywood) as does a fireplace. The feeling of home, family, safety, and security all hover around the hearth. History supports this concept so I'm willing to run with it, and because these memories are so vivid, so cellular, the very presence of a brick-lined box does require we rise to the occasion and support the fantasy in every way possible.

In his deliciously spooky New England tale *The Legend of Sleepy Hollow,* author Washington Irving illustrates this point perfectly. If the sight of a headless horseman weren't jarring enough, the image is made more frightening when we consider the question, "Why is the head missing?" knowing all along that the answer will lead us down eerie paths from which nothing good will ever come.

Our brains register both what is there (horse and rider) and what's not (a head and perhaps a snappy hat). So, it should not be surprising to discover these same feelings when our eyes fall on what should be a perfectly predictable vignette: the hearth and a multitude of necessary implements. Fireplace denotes fire. Fire thrives on a combustible medium. History and experience dictate that wood, in some chopped or sawn form fills this bill

quite nicely. Wood needs to be gathered, bundled, or otherwise organized in a basket or similar container. Then there are the tools with which the wood is manhandled and coaxed into its smoking state of supplication. When the basket or tools are missing, our reasonable expectations are sent packing and the discomfort of this jarring image sends villagers scattering much as does the earlier mentioned horseman.

Regardless of the modern state of your fire box with its gas jets, concrete logs, and remote controls (and yes, there are a multitude of plausible reasons for such installations), you must play along with the expectations a fireplace brings to ensure the greatest comfort and enjoyment for your friends and family. Complete the picture with classic fireplace tools and properly filled wood basket and watch how even the more cynical of your acquaintances warm to the glowing heart of your home.

23 Naked As a Jaybird

While the simile's origin is traced to the nineteenth century when the word jaybird replaced robin, neither word offers much in the way of illumination, other than to draw attention to the bare-assed nature of a thing. Having focused our attention on the naked condition, let's turn our attention to windows—specifically those found in the living room. Much as you would politely pass at the thought of parading into an event wearing your suit of birth, so should you dismiss the concept of the naked window. By their very existence, windows serve certain fundamental purposes. They:

• Allow light to enter a room.

• Invite the circulation of air for the purposes of ventilation.

• Support and enhance the architectural implications of the room.

Since many books explore the point touched on in number three, I will defer to these scholarly tomes and suggest you investigate as your curiosity demands. In our age of fossil fuel dependency and our drive to control as much of our environment as possible the necessity for windows as instruments of ventilation borders on the irrelevant. So let us focus our attention on the magic and marvels of light as understood through the glass of our living room window.

First, a point that often eludes the brightest and the best: when contemplating the line of sight through a pane of glass remember that if you can see them, they can see you. A view of the park or boardwalk or a neighbor's manicured lawn as seen from your living room window is a delight to be sure. Your daylight hours offer resplendent vistas of nature and pedestrians alike all from the safe haven of your home. Let the sun set slowly in the West, however, and wander with me, My Dear Doubting Reader, out your front door, down your front steps, across your

front garden. Then, at the count of three, let's pivot on our spikes like Derek Jeter turning a double play and gaze at your residence from a fresh point of view. Does the word fishbowl float rapidly to the tip of your tongue? Do memories of the zoo (small mammal exhibit) come to mind? Not only does naked apply to the condition of undressed windows viewed from the confines of your home's interior (apartment dwellers pay particular attention) but it also applies to the idea of your life as laid open and bare for all passersby to see.

A second point for consideration: at night, those same bare windows stare back at you like giant black holes, reminding us of spirits of the unfamiliar type intimidating even the most resilient of souls and sucking the life right out of all festivities within their reach. Glass and darkness beyond equals black holes. It is the law (physics and such). While you may have giggled at your grandmoth-

er's layers of shear muslin under her good curtains, there was a thoughtful method to the madness. Not wanting to enclose the room with the weight of the over-curtains made from her favorite damask or chintz, these were left drawn open to frame the window while the sheers (to varying degrees opaque) were drawn like ephemeral veils neutralizing the foreboding gaze of the giant black eyes. It was a simple solution to an unnerving problem. Voilà! Never underestimate the power of a well-placed curtain.

In a perfect world every window would enjoy the covering of a sheer layer and an overcurtain. Alas, the world is not perfect and thus, based on a variety of parameters, there are times when wood blinds, roller shades, shutters, and more are welcome additions on the windows of our homes. Interested in more ideas and options? Visit our website www.101ThingsIHateAboutYourHouse.com.

24 WASTED REAL ESTATE

Honestly assessing the space you possess is the first step toward wise allocation. What dreams do you dream about the home of your dreams? Your fantasy living room may be closer than you think.

Let's cut to the chase, Dear Dazed Reader, it's all about real estate and I hate when it is wasted! If your casa bares uncanny resemblance to the Villa Borghese then you've got real estate aplenty and could allocate a formal room for every erratic swing of a Gemini's mood. I

give you the Sally Field living room with its shades of sappy sunshine yellow touched with resplendent hues of self-aggrandizing turquoise or maybe the Sylvia Plath salon with its greige- and green-draped and valanced windows filtering daylight in layers so depressing it streaks the glass that is veiled by tiered-lace shears weighted with common pond stones. You get the point that when you have space to burn it's easy to waste, but when pressed for every square foot how we use our space begs very specific responses. Few of us suffer from the tedious options inflicted by acres of space. So why waste what you have?

Can you spare space in your home for the formal dining room of your dreams? What of the library, filled to the brim with books of every sort, for which you long? A wise investor in the property might give consideration to a mingling of the minds: a dining room with walls lined with bookshelves makes quick work of both dreams and the realities of your real estate. Be clear and creative with your intentions in any room in your home then, with laserlike focus, remain true to your vision and others will share with you the fruits of this labor of love.

25 A ROOM WITHOUT A SOUL

Little foxes, they have the reputation of spoiling the vines. You know those little foxes, the nuisances that, when left unattended, wreak havoc on things of importance. In the room of living, Dear Ferreter of Foxes (and other troubling life forms), we often are faced with a handful of faux pas that, left unchecked, can leave your guests frustrated and your furniture damaged.

Where, for instance, are the coasters in this room made for living? Often to be pitied is the guest who approaches, sweaty glass in hand, clearly intending to perch on a pouf and join in the riotous conversation. Perching complete, she looks for that small but monumentally important 3½-inch round shield with which she can honor her host and aid in protecting the costly table top on which her dripping drink wants to be placed. Shame on the host who so thoughtlessly neglects this guest in need. It's fair trade, in my opinion, if the French polish on that walnut-marquetry candlestand becomes ghosted and ringed with water spots. Coasters may take shape as sublime artistic triumphs or as kitschy mementoes of errant excursions, but they must exist and they must be on hand at all horizontal surfaces that may tempt a drink into repose.

As the critical eye wanders, yet another flash of fox is revealed and comment is required. Why would one's gaze not spy photographs of family, friends, and the occasional obnoxious but socially essential guest? Where are the personal objects, collections of the heart, the more calculated but nonetheless revealing collections for investment, or childishly sentimental gifts from the youngsters now tucked in their beds? Where, indeed, are the items that distinguish this space from the local hotel lobby or doctor's waiting room? A room that does not reveal some truth about the owner is a room far too sterile for comfort and needs nourishment. Proudly let your slip show. Tell the tale of your household's life through tabletop tableau, and let us learn of your joys and passions. En-

If the gods of decorating are to be found lurking in the details of your home, what do your details say? Take a critical look at the small things that fill your table tops and shelves. Do they tell a beautiful story, the story you want told? If not, then it's time to edit and rewrite your story.

closed cabinets, vitrines, and display cases are best left for your favorite retail destination and their sales quotas. When artfully articulated, the horizontal surfaces in any room (table tops, mantelpieces and bookshelves) make for ideal viewing and the enjoyment of all.

WE ALL KNOW PAYBACK IS A BITCH. So after my rants about your room for living, now it's your turn. Take your best shot (and a few notes) as I share with you my Los Angeles living room. Notice how I've kept things at the windows interesting but unobtrusive (no naked windows here!). Floors are limestone and purposefully left bare. Lamps offer pools of friendly light and the upholstery is comfortable, welcoming, and within easy reach of a variety of tables for drinks and books and such! The art puts a smile on my face; and I've pulled furniture off the wall wherever possible. In the end it's not a bad place to hang out. Tell me what you think and explore my Personal Favorites Resource Center by logging onto www.101ThingsIHateAboutYourHouse.com and becoming a member today.

4

Dining Room

The Way to a Man's (or Woman's) Heart

IT HAS BEEN SAID THAT THE ART OF DINING is a dying art. A case can be made for this proposition; but just as easily, one might take up the optimistic position that reinforces the grace, beauty, and social relevance of the shared meal. Our rooms for dining should hold a vibrant place in our lives and homes. Whether entertaining guests or nurturing those closest to us, this hub of social engagement offers the possibility for dynamic results, infusing our homes and lives with the joys of social connection.

Long ago our predecessors ate their meals around campfires and in caves. These rudimentary feedings gave way to the earliest communal dining experiences, crude as they were. From culture to culture, century to century the breaking of bread has held a pivotal role in the drama of human existence representing, as it has, the highest and lowest forms of social development. The art of the meal, supported by its close cousin conversation, exists to nurture communication, foster hospitality, and support gracious development of the human race. Who knew your decision to feed your family around a hospitable dinner table, supported by stimulating conversation, was integral to the survival of the species. So dine on homemaker, and teach those around you the joys of a well-shared meal. The modern family may not sequester their dining experiences in a room allocated for little else, but dine together they will. Whether in a free-floating space, supporting other household interests, or at a common table in the heart of the kitchen; the art of dining lives on.

26 AN UNBEARABLE CHAIR

Okay children, gather round, I am going to read you a story. It is a monumental saga of love and loss, a story of war and peace, and of life and death slung out through the generations. While I read all 927 pages, aloud, slowly, I'd like for you to perch your boney little behinds on these wood slats with little back support all teetering on spindly legs and, while you do that, remember you should be well-dressed, engaging, and play well with those around you. Sounds like fun, doesn't it? Well, of course not. I would rather have dental surgery than sit through this tedious exercise. How many brunches, luncheons, and dinner parties have we suffered through in chairs none too dis-similar to these, as if selected (if

The limitations of the human body are such that comfort will always trump good intentions. Make the job of a guest in your home easy by providing the greatest comfort possible. Your guests will thank you and your praises will be sung both far and wide.

not designed) by the Marquis de Sade himself?

In reflecting on his inevitable nap during Sunday morning services, my grandfather maintained, "The mind can only absorb what the seat can endure." As the morning sermon droned on, Grandpa's mind lost the battle to his "seat" of learning and the requisite nap, to the delight of his grandchildren, was born. In light of this, know that all the fashionable festivities packed into your next fete will fall on dulled brains if you haven't made certain that other weightier (theirs, not ours) matters are gently caressed, pampered, and cushioned.

Consider if you will the merits of upholstered dining chairs. When faced with the prospect of rigid plastic or tufted velvet, which would you choose? In pondering your answer to this question, Dear Recumbent Reader, I beg of you one thing; forget for a moment your status as a card-carrying modernist, professing in zealous tones the virtues of form over function. Instead, consider the general description of the dining chair in which you were last seen so lost in the heady weave of food, wine, and conversation that you lingered, without disfiguring injury, in a dining chair for hours. Personal experience has shown that the dining tables I linger at with the greatest ease are those supported by comfortably upholstered chairs.

27 LUDICROUS LIGHTING

Dear Gentle Reader, as we scamper down the path of history and glance briefly at the evolution of dining two things stand out: We have forgone the quaint use of our hands as dining instruments (praise be!). We have evolved our technical capacity for illumination beyond the wall hung torches and laborious chandeliers found in the dining halls of sixteenth-century Europe.

Not to say that we cannot learn from our early, if crude, ancestors; let's toss a couple of concepts on the table for consideration. First, there's general lighting. Think giant, hammered-iron monstrosities suspended high above the great hall with knobby candles plopped down on sturdy steel arms casting uneven light. This unsteady glow, cast from high above, coats the room with a blanket of dappled honey-colored light. An effect that was perfectly fine if you needed to avoid walking into the side of the dining table, but less successful when trying to find the eyehook on your chain-mail frock coat. Second, there's task lighting. With specific duties at hand, practical solutions were required. Seeing what was set before them on long banquet tables required a light source much closer to the user and to items considered for consumption. Candelabra (torch on stand) came into being. Moving from one location in the castle to another required navigating hallways and passages. Illumination seemed like a good idea so our ancestors hung torches from brackets and placed them at helpful intervals down the dank, dark hallways. Inviting, maybe not, but at least you could avoid running into walls, knights, or the wrong end of a sword.

Dear Receiver of Illumination, as a rule, hang your chandelier thirty-six inches above the top of your dining table, pop in maximum 25-watt frosted bulbs, no flame tips please, and, of course, add a stylish shade of your choosing. Generally, this allows for both a successful relationship between source and subject and through the magic of dimming, ideal light for every dining experience. You will look good as you always want to be seen in the best light possible. Your guests should glow beautifully, though they should never look as good as you. The table (your creative masterpiece) should be washed in light to make Caravaggio weep.

And yes, selecting a perfectly divine chandelier helps. Finding one with an appropriate number of candles for the room size is important. (Generally one candlestick per seated guest with four as a minimum.) Sheared over the chain in a subtle harmonious fabric, the cord sleeve helps the cause but, at the end of the day, if you've hung the chandelier so high that your guests strain to catch a glimpse of it, don't be surprised when they topple over, unable now to compliment you on your stunning antique selection. You might as well have bought the lacquered brass number from Big Pete's Lights and Appliances and called it a day. *SHREEK!*

Now a word on candles: yes! Use them often and everywhere. Pertinent to this discussion, use them on your table. When combined with dimmed light from a marvelously hung chandelier the light from candles will make for a most beautiful dining experience.

28 STAGGERING CENTERPIECES

Imagine with me, my Dear Harvester of Hospitable Knowledge, the sensation a guest in your humble manor experiences when seated at your table. First, let us not forget the honor such seating and the preceding invitation carries. To be a guest in a home is a weighty matter and carries with it rights and responsibilities. Despite volumes written on the subject, many people cannot fathom the nuances attached to their role as a guest. Suffice it to say, as host you have bestowed on this transient mortal the honor of suffering through your blossoming efforts at noble hospitality. They have navigated the minefield of your cocktail hour, managing to neither offend nor be offended by the random cast you have gathered for this high and holy event. Now comes the moment that all moments anticipate. Now is the time when said guest is delivered to the high alter of entertaining: the dining table.

Set with ceremonial precision by the Vestal Virgins, the table itself can be a feast for all the senses. But, this feast can quickly become Nero's dungeon if the table is set up in a manner that does not encourage conversation. Lively, dare we say stimulating, conversation is the appropriate sacrifice to be presented. Reluctantly we settle, most often, for the occasional complete sentence. Sparkling conversation is a worthy offering for a guest to present, doing honor to his host and making his presence important and worth repeating. Death and doldrums are in store for any dinner event when conversation is hindered. Shame on the host who, with careless disregard for supplications prepared by guests, stifles conversation through the inept layout of the room of dining. Conversations cannot take place when boxwood hedges pose as centerpieces. In much the same way, vessels piled high with buds and branches impede even the most well-intended social exchange.

While vast improvements to the world of silk flowers have been made, these are best left to commercial situations and not for regular use in our homes.

CENTERPIECE SENSE

When contemplating the makeup of the center of your table, focus on this short list of failure-proof ideas:

FRESH-CUT FLOWERS. Focus attention on your favorite species; and whether you purchase and arrange the flowers yourself or hire out the services of a local floral talent, keep the arrangements low and luxurious.

POTTED FLOWERS. Orchids, azaleas, tulips, and begonias are just a few delightful options that, when dotted down the center of your table, make natural elegance second nature.

GREENERY. Evergreen, citrus, magnolia, and grasses all can be woven into glorious focal points for tables of all sizes and occasions.

And let's look, just for a moment, at the tennis-match quality of conversation required by the elongated table of dining. Unless "stiff" and "formal" are your desired results, Dear Host of the High Alter, consider "low" and "round" as you ponder the centerpiece and table respectively. Common sense and the laws of physics dictate that the shortest distance between two points is a straight line. The lines connecting guests at a round table form a lovely fabric of congeniality. As round is not always an option, do your very best to keep all other impediments from cropping up between your guests.

29   THE BOWLING ALLEY BLUES

If forced to be truthful, each of us will admit to a slight preference for the sound of our own voice. There is no shock or shame attached to this observation. Often we're the only one within earshot making two-cents worth of sense, so why wouldn't we enjoy our own musings? Even I draw the line in this theater of me at the prospect of hearing my voice stretched, twisted, and shot back at me in repetitive waves. In short, I hate an echo. Let me repeat, I hate an echo. Echoes are charming, in a Cecil B. DeMille kind of way, when part of a Swiss mountain postcard scene. Heidi's braids are quivering and everyone knows the reverberation of her voice off

the Matterhorn causes the bounce. How sweet. How cute. No one looks *that* good in lederhosen.

Nor does anyone sound good when their crisp, practiced inflection is garbled by "the repetition of a sound caused by reflection of sound waves," which helpful *Webster* defines as an echo. We are most susceptible to "reflections" when hard surfaces are present and never are hard surfaces more present than in the expanse known as the dining room. Between the tabletop, regularly constructed of wood, stone, or glass, and the floor on which the table stands, invariably made of wood, or stone, or an artful combination of the two, we have a smorgasbord of sound bouncing surfaces.

Hate noisy restaurants? Don't let their mistakes become yours. Generous use of sound absorbing surfaces will keep noise levels in your dining room at comfortable levels. Area rugs, curtains, and a beautifully draped dining table all go far toward controlling the levels of noise your joyful guests must endure.

One might ponder the question: "Why did the Titanic hit that giant ice cube?" The answer is quite simple; no one knew it was there. Alas, the tragedy of ignorance. It is much the same for you—until today. Your days of wandering among the deafening echo of your dining room are over. Get thee to a rug store, an emporium of antique carpets, or the nearest tag sale, and find something lovely to lay under your feet.

The size of your newfound prize should, at a minimum, be 36 inches larger on all four sides than the dining table lying beneath. And a nonskid pad under the carpet will keep guests from slipping and cluttering your floor in an awkward and unhealthy manner. Points are awarded for beauty and bonus points for practicality and function as you enjoy the hush your new addition brings your hall of dining.

30 A THOUGHTLESS LAY

Whether set for guests or the daily droves, what you place on your table rends the veil exposing the inner workings of your head and heart. Lest you kid yourself into believing otherwise, the manner in which you set your table is the domus equivalent of the Rorschach test. Fear and loathing, paranoia and clinical depression, jealousy and sublimated rage, and phobias galore announce their existence by what you choose to place on your table. Not every home requires sterling silver nor do hours need be spent measuring the placements at each place setting—but please, care enough to take pride in how your table is laid. Yes, it's a daily chore, but those of you with children, consider engaging this built-in labor force. With a bit of training in the fundamentals, you can unleash their creative souls with the most interesting and inspired results. And yes, it requires a bit of preparation (those interesting flatware patterns or vintage serving pieces don't materialize in your cabinets on their own). You may also want to fire up an additional imaginative brain cell or two by broadening your vocabulary on the subject. Roll up your sleeves and invest some time and energy. You will undoubtedly reap rewards as you discover the varied ways in which you, I mean your table, can get laid.

The successfully set table draws on your ever-growing collection of china, crystal, flatware, and interesting objects and containers. For the best deals, the collector's quest should include local tag and garage sales, second-hand shops, regional antique fairs, and specialty dealers. You don't need to spend tons of money; shop smart and have fun.

TABLE-SETTING BASICS

A discussion of the art associated with setting a beautiful table would fill a book of its own. We'll focus here on five tips for a beautiful table.

A GOOD FOUNDATION. Wood tabletops by their very nature require a cloth or mats to protect their surfaces. You can dress up or down either option in your choice of materials. When draping a table always use a felt table liner; the cloth will lie more beautifully, and your table will be better protected.

TOOLS OF THE TRADE. Buy it yourself (favorite retailer, antique dealer, or tag sale) or snag a set through marriage or other gift receiving endeavor, but start your table setting adventure with one good set of dishes. Your choices are vast and you're encouraged to add additional sets as time goes by. I suggest a very nice set of white china as a stellar starting point. Bold patterns and exciting colors make good secondary sets for use when you're spicing things up. Mixing and matching is a cautionary tale; gorgeous when done well, sad the rest of the time. Establish a beautifully consistent track record before you experiment or raise the bar in this manner.

MORE TOOLS OF THE TRADE. Flatware and crystal drinkware should be approached in the same manner; one good set for daily use, supported by a lifetime of satellite acquisitions. Sterling flatware is beautiful, but requires regular maintenance. Silver plate is best for daily use. Stainless steel may be easier on your budget. Regardless of the material, make certain there is an ample substance to the material. Nothing feels cheaper than featherweight flatware. Ditto for glassware at your table of dining; select nicely weighted pieces in a pattern that complements your dinnerware. A variety of wine glasses (for reds and whites to start with), water, and cocktail tumbler options make up a host's basic entertaining arsenal. Purchasing from well-established manufacturers makes adding to your collection over time a simple matter.

SERVICE MATTERS. Serving platters, trays, and dishes round out the pantry of well-prepared hosts or hostesses. Keep your shopper's eyes peeled for these wonderful additions; coordinate colors and materials with your primary set of dishes, but never hesitate to snap-up something of interest. There's always room for something beautiful.

COURTING CENTER. Time and experience in your dining room will best prepare you to collect appropriate and interesting containers for use in the centerpieces you create. Cream ware, pottery, glassware and silver are only starting points for this constantly expanding collection. Don't be shy; collect what you love.

31 Dining on My Feet

When you can't see the forest for the trees maybe it's time to come indoors. It now seems like a good time to part the Red Sea and walk on water, all at the same time. I want to get your attention because I know there are people out there who:

- Believe there is no need for a dining room.
- Know for a fact (presumably) that there is no space for a dining room.

For those who believe the dining room shares with the dinosaurs the status of extinction, allow me one question. Where, exactly, do you and your family partake of meals? I'm just curious. Possibly you dine in the breakfast room (small space often adjoining the kitchen), at the kitchen counter (barstools and all), or on trays appropriately labeled "TV" for their obvious connection. There are no wrong answers to this question. But for most responses that I can muster the following truths still hold:

- More than one person participates.
- These people are gathering to share a nourishing meal.
- It is possible, even hopeful, that some form of communication may be involved.
- Guests (those not currently living in the house) may share in the experience.

Even if your idea of fine dining includes a delivery boy and plastic utensils, allow me to stir your heart and challenge your thinking. If the only consideration presented by this subject was the consumption of food then I would have already designed a standing trough-like apparatus from which families could shovel their grub and run. For centuries, dining has provided the opportunity for an experience, a prized venue for communication, education, illumination, and negotiation—all of which have advanced the state of the human race in ways we cannot easily ignore. By diminishing the general tone of your daily dining experience to that of "swallow and dash," you are depriving yourself of a large part of the excitement and satisfaction of life. If you are going to the dance, then you might as well plan on dancing! Don't you think?

For those longing for the opportunity to set a beautiful table but find themselves short on real estate it's time to think outside the box. At times, I mean this literally. For those of us living in temperate climates, the possibility of alfresco dining exists during the appropriate seasons. A terrace, balcony, lawn, or garden can offer entertaining opportunities that may feed your dining desires when the confine of your abode so strongly objects. If you are locked inside, then let's look inward at the surprising options that exist. You can slip a folding table, a gate-leg table, or your parents' card table into even the snuggest of interiors and create an intimate dining experience. Move the cocktail table, slide back the sofa, empty your entry hall, or even (yes, I've seen it done with wit and grace) set a table in your bedroom. If entertaining (even if it's dinner for you and your sweetheart) is important to you, use your imagination for all your worth and come up with a creative solution for your unique challenge. Then take a picture and e-mail it to me. I would love to see your mind at work!

32 NO HUTCH IN SIGHT

"A place for everything and everything in its place" is a concept shared, by linear minds, down through the ages. What a wonderful thought that by simply putting everything away you have helped resolve one of the universe's small quandaries. What preparations have you made in your dining room for the storage of china, crystal, and flatware? Breakfronts, buffets, cabinets, and hutches all point you in the right direction when thoughts turn to storage. As is always the case in cases (or cabinets) like this, you will fill whatever space you carve out. Give yourself a lot of space and you will find yourself with a lot of stuff. Limit your available space and you will limit your possessions. If you secure a sideboard or buffet in which to house your dining utensils you gain a surface from which to serve or display—two points for your team. Don't allow the whims of fashion or fad to dissuade you from owning pieces like this, for the "win" is always worth the fight.

33 PAPER NAPKINS

I cringe at the thought of the dripping, limp remnants of the paper napkin that has relentlessly applied itself to the side of my cocktail glass on too-numerous occasions. Right up there with someone else's snotty handkerchief, this ghost of a napkin always makes me want to wash my hands. The paper cocktail napkin's cousin (however nicely monogrammed it may be), the paper dinner napkin, far too often relinquishes its fighting spirit, and this usually happens just in time to jeopardize a favorite suit or skirt. There are many situations when the use of paper products makes sense. Picnics, barbeques, and poolside romps easily top the list along with family dinners that include young children. Beyond these situations, I always prefer to bother with cotton or linen napkins. Yes, I know it involves a lot of work: washing, starching, ironing, and storing. The result is worth the effort. The touch, the feel, the class—well, you get the idea.

Cloth napkins are not as scary as you think. Purchase cotton or linen, wash in warm water using your washer's gentle cycle, tumble until damp dry, give a shot of spray starch, and a once-over-both-sides with a hot steam iron. Fold, stack, then wrap each freshly pressed stack with a colored grosgrain ribbon and tuck in a sprig of lavender.

Sparkle as a host or hostess with a collection of cloth napkins coordinating with or matching your tablecloth or place mats.

HERE'S A LOOK AT A CLIENT'S DINING ROOM; one that hits the high points of gracious and beautiful entertaining. From the rug on the floor (my design) to the comfortable reproduction dining chairs, to the layers of curtains on the windows to the orchid centerpiece on the Charles X dining table, all topped off by a charmingly shaded chandelier, this room is ready for any entertaining situation. How does your room for dining stack up? I'd love to hear from you so log onto our website, send me a picture, a comment, or question. And while you're at it explore more of my Personal Favorites Resource Center.

5

Kitchen

IF THE ROOM FOR DINING IS THE HUB of a home's social life then, certainly, the kitchen can be considered the center of family life. Beauty and practicality are the directives laid out for this, the heart of the home. A tall order for any room, but both desired and necessary as it is from this space that entertaining impulses emanate and all things social have their base. Get this right and a tone of gracious hospitality is set for all to enjoy.

Starting with early man's open fire, the location for food preparation has been pivotal in developing the manner in which we live. Gone are the days when kitchens occupied the lower levels of a house, out-of-sight and out-of-mind until hunger stirred and food materialized. Today the pendulum has swung to another extreme placing the heart of the house on display for all to see. For better or worse, the kitchens of today often function as showrooms offering the secrets of the hearth as fodder for comment and contemplation. Cooking in a fishbowl presents particular challenges when the whole of the entertaining experience is considered. So whether you're laid bare for the world to see or hidden behind closed doors, kitchens of today offer great challenges and rewards. Get it right and your house ticks away like a runner's heart pumping life through the veins of your home. Get it wrong and the atrophy of poor design decisions will be felt in the farthest corners of the attic, basement, and everything in between. So perk up, take some notes, and make your kitchen dazzle.

34 AN OPEN FLOOR PLAN

Dear Ferreter of the Fashionable, Oh Lady/Lad of Luxury tell me truly, when last did you make an entrance at a very important function (Brava!) followed by a skillful stroll through the crowd only to arrive at the center of the room and begin stripping off your overpriced yet highly prized couture. Heels, handbag, hose, and more—all slung on the floor exposing for the world to see the minor "helpers" used to pull your great look together (duck tape, underwire, support tops, optical mirrors, etc.). "Well I never"

would be the correct response to this crazy notion. However, think about this: essentially, you do the same thing when you entertain in your home and you toss open the heart of the house (fount of all secrets and surprises), otherwise known as the kitchen, for the entire world to see.

Yes, salmon swim upstream, and I am certain a svelte figure is a happy by-product of their determination, which is much how I feel when voicing thoughts on this subject (pray to the gods of thunder that I'm cursed with that svelte problem).

The wide, laborious stream of populous opinion seems poised to deposit the kitchen of today into the middle of the entry hall. If I want to greet my guests from a perch at my Hansgrohe accented sink, I could just as easily ask them to use the back door and be done with the formalities. I could also ask them to bring their own folding chairs and a box of their favorite wine. Odds are these things won't happen.

I am well aware that the role of host/hostess is synonymous with that of the overachiever. The lines blur and we strain for the superpowers that allow us to deal with the con-

The open kitchen: love it or hate it, but it's here to stay. The idea of a kitchen closed to the rest of the house seems old-fashion when considered alongside the majority of wide-open spaces offered by developers today. Make your open kitchen sparkle with a touch of organization. A place for everything and everything in its place.

tractors, the gardeners, the decorator (smooth as silk, just like "buttah"), the pool boy (I said nothing), the school crosswalk attendant, the parking attendant, the receptionist, the assistant, the boss, the client, the florist, the manicurist, the hairstylist, the boutique clerk, the shoe repairman (save my Blahniks, please), the deejay, the parking staff, the housekeeper, the kids, and the spouse—all the day of the dinner

party. Add to that cooking, serving, and cleaning as you go, while twelve of your nearest and dearest, smelling of slow gin and an even slower luncheon, slip into their new Zac Posens and through your front door ready for entertainment.

The last thing I would want at that moment is the heat of the oven, over which I am hovering, to melt the last hint of glue on my eyelashes and send my upswept 'do cascading down my neck like so much wet spaghetti. I'm stretched to my limit when I must be charming, entertaining, smart, and sexy while stirring a vat of boiling water, pouring drinks, and basting a dish in a sweltering oven while hawking freshly coiffed canapés from trays of woven new-growth bamboo. I want to hide, to be shielded, buffered, or, at bare minimum, to know my escape is just through that door. The door to the kitchen, that is. Boys, put a door where a door wants to be, and I say a door wants to be between my kitchen and the rest of my home.

OPEN KITCHEN TIPS

If the walls of your casa simply won't oblige (and a major remodel is out of the question) do not fear. Keep these three tips in mind when entertaining your family or friends. Yes, it takes a bit more planning and a teensy bit more work, but your reputation as a godlike host or hostess is well worth the effort.

CLEAN AS YOU GO. Gone are the days of letting every pot and pan you own pile high in the sink as you wait for guests to depart. Corral the kids into scullery duty before the guests arrive, and start your event with a miraculously clean and open kitchen. The whispers of your superhuman entertaining powers will precede you.

ADJUST YOUR MENU. Slaving in the kitchen for days on end seems a quaint idea at best. No one has the time or, it seems, the inclination these days. So structure your menu in a streamlined manner and prepare your efficient meals primarily in advance. You'll enjoy more of your own party and your kitchen will dazzle.

ASSIMILATE AND CONQUER. If your wide open spaces allow and your menu demands a more hands-on approach, why not bring the mountain to Muhammad. Think casual and interactive for your next dinner party; just move the whole thing around your kitchen bar or island. Host your very own cooking extravaganza and put the crowd to work. With enough laughter and wine no one will notice the dirty dishes in the sink. In fact, if you're a real take-charge type put one of your guests to work washing dishes. They'll either beat down your door wanting to do it all over or you'll never hear from them again. A dull pack of losers are they if the latter is the case. My money is on a grand time being had by all.

35 SIZE SNOBS

To dwellers of the city, I tip my hat. Forced by the facts of city life, which read like a Lilliputian manifesto, they make miracles happen from kitchens no larger than closets. Only small thinking people write off tiny kitchens as untenable. Annoying is the arrogance of suburbanites who believe acres of space are required for entertaining excellence. Nothing could be further from the truth and this wee story should help to make my case.

City dwellers divide and conquer, divide again, only to have to conquer again with one foot in the coat closet and the other in the guest's claw-foot bathtub, but, dammit, they conquer.

Recently, while hovering near the "terrace" (for those in the middle states this is more readily recognized as the fire escape) in a dear friend's Midtown masterpiece (i.e., junior studio awash with floor-to-ceiling mirrors) I was dumbstruck (and that, Kittens of Copious Consumption, doesn't happen often) by the contortions going on in the kitchen/guest closet/wrapping room.

Great things come in small packages, kitchens included. A small overall space doesn't mean you must sacrifice efficiency. Top-of-the-line, small-scale appliances can make even the smallest space function like a full-size kitchen.

Teetering on a killer Manolo heel (yes, one), our hostess balanced a tray of freshly toasted brioche in one hand while scanning a text message on her mobile that was commandingly perched on top of her teeny-tiny-but-definitely-not-under-the-counter refrigerator (think eyelash-level), while reaching, with her free hand, for the freshly chopped olive and anchovy tapenade.

Her free and fabulously shod foot had just kicked closed the oven door (from whence the brioche came) and was flying toward me at an alarming speed in an attempt to prevent an empty tumbler—launched from the lecherous paws of a party "crasher" as he reached for the fetchingly fit fanny of some upper West Side ad executive—from shattering on the stone entry floor (one 12-inch by 12-inch tile really doesn't an entry hall make, but big points for trying).

After that nifty save, this hostess has a "buy" from me. The woman can do no wrong. Remarkably the tumbler (Granny's Baccarat) and the free-flying Manolo both survived without a dint, ding, or chip. Praise be! The moral to this story is never write off a small kitchen as being incapable of producing dazzling feats of entertainment. Big things come in small packages, and at the end of the day it's not size that matters but what you do with what you've got!

36) WHEN TOO MUCH IS TOO MUCH

There may be a segment of those reading this book, Dear Readers of Ribaldry, for whom my next statement will be scandalous. Humor me and resist the temptation of chucking the text into the nearest open fire. Together we can get through this, I promise. There are times when the kitchen is just too big. Following a developer-driven trend toward stadium-size kitchens, many in our land are laden down with acres of space in their cooking zones. If this is what the decorating gods have dealt you, then make good use of what you've got even if Rollerblades are required. If you're planning a new kitchen in the home of your dreams, give careful consideration to what your real needs are as opposed to those suggested by the building trades. They are not necessarily one and the same.

Remember just because something can be supersized doesn't mean it should be. The menus at our nation's fast food establishments underscore this point perfectly. I like a good hamburger now and then but, when did we decide that a 1,500 calorie hamburger was something anyone actually needs to consume?

When contemplating things that have become too large, it would be foolish to ignore the recent financial meltdown. Interwoven with the unraveling of major corporations we found a phrase used to describe the behemoths: we were told they are "too big to fail," but in hindsight we now might say we were told wrong. Bigger doesn't seem like such a great idea any more.

So in a quest for cozy here are a few tricks to consider as you look to distract from your culinary acreage and enhance the charm as best you can. First, learn to control your lighting controls and with a flip of a switch take your kitchen from appearing like an overly lit stadium to that of a softer, warmer, more intimate space. Next, fill the space with people. You'll feel less like Alice in Wonderland and more like the belle of the ball when you've got friends and family swirling about you laughing, working, and generally enjoying themselves.

37 A GROUTED-TILE COUNTERTOP

There are many things in this life that I will never fully understand. I have made peace with this deficit and, despite many who believe I possess all knowledge as well as great amounts of wisdom, I welcome the load this understanding has lifted.

When pondering the many choices that go into building a successful kitchen one option completely eludes me. First, let me say in regard to monumental issues in life, every choice is a compromise. There is no magic solution that will address every concern with perfection. This recognition opens a wide and often confusing process of exploration that regularly dogs the steps of home owners. Product and material choices abound often to the point of distraction.

Clairvoyance, or experience, is the only hope for salvation. Fueled purely by experience, as my skills as a clairvoyant are lacking in the extreme, here are my thoughtful thoughts. Let's talk counters.

Stone, tile, and fabricated materials are the broad categories from which all selections for countertops are made. Stone is drawn from the wonders of Mother Nature. Don't mess with the mistress of creation. When you want something of great beauty go for marble, limestone, or granite. Cost of materials and labor to fabricate and install must be considered. The only way to know for sure how much this will cost is to select a stone you love and have a contractor provide a quote. You can learn more about my preferred stone selections along with pro's and con's of alternate choices at my Personal Favorites Resource Center found at www.101ThingsIHate AboutYourHouse.com. Remember the most beautiful product choices are appropriate to your needs, your home's architecture, and your budget. But for ease of daily use, beauty, and a long happy life, some type of stone is at the top of my list.

Laminates cover the other end of the spectrum offering great cost effectiveness and a complete lack of natural beauty. At times, given the cost implications, laminate can be a most effective solution, particularly if you choose the solid color products (color of top layer of plastic runs through the entire product eliminating the black seam typical of a laminate installation.

Tile is our final consideration. Often beautiful, tile offers a range of colors, patterns, and textures that provide end-less inspirational possibilities. Tile, however, by its very nature, requires the presence of grout to seal the deal. In my estimation, the introduction of a grouted surface on a countertop (very different from its use on the backsplash) is like customizing your own little petri dish, then evenly distributing it across the entire counter surface of your kitchen. You'll experience daily stains and spend most of your waking hours with toothbrush in hand trying to stave off the inevitable results of introducing grout into a kitchen.

Just a note about your backsplash; first it should always fully extend to the underside of your upper cabinets. Four or six inches of backsplash makes it look like you ran out of product, patience, money, or all the above. It's always appropriate to use your countertop material

for backsplash. If you long for tile in your kitchen of dreams, a backsplash is the place for it, as grout stains are less likely on this vertical surface. If cost is a concern, mirroring your backsplash can be a chic, stylish, and highly effective selection. Durable and easy to clean, it adds to the perceived size of your kitchen through the magic of mirror.

38 A Crystal Chandelier

Needless to say, lighting is important to create a functional kitchen. What is simply not important to the life and success of your hearth of the home, Dear Radiant Reader, is a crystal chandelier. Just don't do it. I know you've seen them splashed across the pages of glossy, four-color shelter magazines and I suppose the word "splashed" would sum up my criticism nicely. Kitchens are by their very nature messy places. Grease and oil, to name just a few flying elements in most any active kitchen, end up touching most every surface. No doubt, you do keep your kitchen impeccably clean; a process that takes no small amount of time and energy. Who wants or needs to clean each piece of rock crystal from that wonderful eighteenth-century French flourish that illuminates your primary workspace? While at first glance the grandiose glam of a chandelier may seem beautiful, but look a bit closer, and the layers of grease and grime exponentially diminish any beauty

associated with this disastrous decorating demonstration.

But light a kitchen we must, and here are a few things to keep in mind when tackling this task. General or ambient light is a must. Will it be a combination of recessed ceiling cans, surface-mounted lights, or hanging fixtures? With many options available and each kitchen different, this becomes a very personal search with the goal to produce the most even general lighting possible. While local municipalities may require fluorescent bulbs to pass code, living with these can be a challenge—for there is no less forgiving light on the planet than that of a standard fluorescent bulb. Technology does march on and we're told that changes are afoot. Pray to the decorating gods this is so; otherwise steer clear.

Undercounter lighting is a must but shop wisely for an appropriate product. Puck lights and undercounter cans illuminate, but produce hot spots with uneven, overlapping circles. In a word: ugly. Strip lights or rope lights offer a better option and cast a consistent band of light. Much more pleasant to live and work with. These selections need to be woven into the construction of your

Each kitchen requires a unique approach to illumination to meet the demand for task, ambient, and general lighting. Log onto our resource center at www.101ThingsIHateAboutYourHouse.com and take our kitchen lighting test. Then use our resource center to discover new lighting options that add style, value, and function to your kitchen.

cabinetry so consult a professional for these to be installed correctly. With under-the-counter lighting in place, any additional illuminators can be considered decorative; so go knock yourself out, but remember our earlier caveat regarding crystal in the kitchen and just say no.

If fabric is out, what's a homemaker to use on the walls and windows of the kitchen? Microfibers offer amazing resiliency and the beauty of more delicate materials. Whether in woven form or paperbacked, microfibers can be applied to the walls. You'll find a wide range of color and texture in these state-of-the-art products. Match this with woven shades on your windows for a sophisticated look.

39   YARDS AND YARDS OF FABRIC

Dear Fair Reader, simply put: if it is fabric ("A material that resembles cloth" that Webster goes on to define as "a pliable material made usually by weaving, felting, or knitting natural or synthetic fibers and filaments") then its only place in the kitchen is as a beautifully woven, possibly monogrammed tea towel. You would no more set up a hot plate or deep fryer in your walk-in closet than you would light a match to your wardrobe. So why would you go to all the trouble of hanging equally valuable fabric anywhere in your kitchen, and have any expectation

other than its complete and total destruction. Unless you don't cook and wish your kitchen to look like a set piece, I highly recommend avoiding the use of fabric anywhere near your food preparation area. Rely instead on either a painted finish (eggshell or semi-gloss work well) in a color of your selecting or a wall covering that allows for its surface to be scrubbed clean. Technology being what it is today, there are many stunning wall coverings available that you can spray and wipe. A mother's prayer is answered.

40 Glass-Fronted Cabinets

Just like the tot who raised his voice inquiring, with simple honesty, why the Emperor was marching down the boulevard in his birthday suit; so, too, must I raise the strikingly simple question, "Why do your cabinets interiors look like the sales tables at Filene's Basement?" Now, if you had installed solid fronts on your cabinet doors you could quickly and successfully dismiss my comment as the ramblings of some uninvited, drunken guest and ask if you could call me a cab. However, since you just had to have those glass-paneled, upper-cabinet doors you can hardly act too demure without looking like a naked monarch. The math is simple, Dear Overly Exposed Reader, if glass cabinet doors are what you want, then be prepared to maintain a level of orderliness. Otherwise, straighten up the shelves or smash the glass and start over. Either way you'll be on your way to a more beautiful kitchen.

41 Kitchen Clutter

Regardless of glass-fronted or solid wood cabinets, your kitchen requires some method or system of organization and storage to succeed. Food stuffs, pots and pans, dishes, and utensils all ben-

efit from a framework of organization. The absence of such a system leaves anarchy reigning and frustration for everyone. Follow, instead, this simple organizational primer. Stand at one of the three key action centers found in every kitchen. The sink (and by extension dishwasher), the cooktop and ovens, and the refrigerator. Orient yourself in relation to the tasks preformed at each station. Now begin prioritizing the storage of cookware and utensils, spices and seasonings, flatware, serving pieces, and so on until you've accounted for all the items in your daily culinary vocabulary. Consider ease of access as well as storage. Some find that storing daily dishware in lower cabinets on pullout shelves makes more sense when unloading from a nearby dishwasher.

42   Talking Trash

Much like the little game of "hide the waste can" we played in the powder room, in the kitchen we move up to the major leagues. In today's kitchen we have trash; we have wet trash, dry trash, compostable trash, recyclable trash, refundable trash, and biodegradable trash. We have created new industries around the handling of trash (with good intention and growing accountability), but we are often ill prepared to manage the point of origin—our own kitchens. Gone are the days when the trash was under the kitchen sink. Today you need a ten-foot run of cabinetry to successfully "cabinet-ize" trash storage. If you're not ready to remodel your kitchen, making it trash coordination central, then you need to put plan "B" in place, which allows you to be responsible but falls short of filling all available kitchen and laundry room floor space with blue recycling bins. This arrangement can be fun for the kids and dogs but a disaster for anyone over 40-inches tall.

The brightest and the best might co-opt a slice of space in the garage and install "recycle central," complete with enough big blue bins to turn anyone positively green! Or you may choose to allocate space in your laundry room or mud room. As important to our environment as this disciplined ap-

Explore smart, stylish options for your personal recycling headquarters at our resource center at www.101Things IHateAboutYourHouse.com.

proach to trash and recyclable disposal is, you must find a sensible solution within your own four walls. Sacrificing family sanity for the sake of a few recycling bins is hardly a deal worth brokering. Look for product ideas at My Personal Favorite Resource Center www.101ThingsIHateAboutYourHouse.com. Happy recycling.

43 AN APPLIANCE GRAVEYARD

"Be a kid at heart" is an admonition that rings true for young and old alike. The young can't imagine being any other way and the old are determined to keep the bounce in their head and heart for as long as is possible. What picture of childhood is complete without toys littering the ground as far as the eye can see? Toys sparkle and intrigue, allowing their owner to fudge reality and, for a moment, align themselves with these beautifully packaged diversions. Toys are not allocated just to children as a glance at some mega-kitchens will prove. Do you really need that gelato maker? A cappuccino machine? A bread maker? I'm enthralled with the thought of a kitchen filled to the brim with tools necessary for creating joyful memories so if you use the gadgets, gizmos, and contraptions by all means store them conveniently in an appliance garage, cabinet, or nearby pantry. I'm much less fond of a kitchen that has become a graveyard for obsolete adult toys. Keep it young but keep it real.

Take a peek at this Massachusetts farmhouse kitchen. The house dates back to 1790 and let me tell you it's one thing to fill a house with antiques, another thing entirely to live in one! Historical preservation being what it is (and I do applaud all the great efforts along these lines), working within a protected property is enough to make you curse all old things! But we prevailed and whipped up a charming little kitchen for a growing family. Viking appliances eased the way into the twenty-first century though we had no space for a dishwasher. Since walls could not be moved, we held no hope of making room so we dolled up the sink area where lots of wash'in and dry'in was set to take place. A black and white tile floor, painted walls and cabinetry were wonderful foils for the soapstone counters. One extravagance came in the form of a marble-topped Charles X buffet, which helped ease the otherwise cramped storage space. I think it all made for a winning little kitchen in a big old house.

6

Family Room

No One Gets Left Behind

THE SIMPLE TRUTH ABOUT FAMILY is that we all have one, either by birth or choice. Our birth family may have offered us warmth, safety, and nurturing or may have failed us and left us abandoned, either physically or emotionally. Enter the family of choice. This would be the group of our nearest and dearest friends, who we draw close and who provides us with a sense of belonging. Beginning in the mid-twentieth century, architects and developers, eager to distinguish their suburban track-home product from other

homes, began promoting the idea of a central gathering room, separate from the more formal living room. The family room was born, resplendent with sectional sofas, console televisions, and TV trays. Wood paneling seemed to make its way into the mix more often than not and, as time moved forward, the ubiquitous wall-to-wall shag carpet covered the floors. With historical roots in private sitting rooms of the late-nineteenth- and early-twentieth-century homes, where one might gather one's family and closest of friends for informal gatherings, today's family room has emerged as the hub of familial activities.

44 UNCOMFORTABLE FURNITURE

Just like your favorite sweatshirt, the family room's comfort level is of foremost concern. Of what good or purpose, other than to cool your contemporary jets, are rigidly upholstered, leather-clad sofas and chairs? Even the most abstract idea of this room for family falls short when comfort (physical, emotional, and spiritual) is sold short for edgy style or dramatic effect. On the great stage of life if family is the cast then the room of gathering is one where characters, costumes, and layers of stage makeup are vanquished in favor of the real you. So take a look at your upholstery. If, when contemplating said upholstery, the urge to curl up with a good book never crosses your mind then "Katy bar the door!"

45 Out-of-Control Pillows

Applaud you, I will, for dashing out and snatching up decorative pillows of glorious fabric and delicious trim. The applause will swell as you cart home these new finds and pile them on the sofas and chairs of your familial chamber.

Thunderous will be the accolades showered on you when you cut loose of your panicked need to protect your new acquisitions, unchain the family from their tethers, and allow them to flop and romp and generally enjoy themselves on the pillow-enhanced upholstery. Dead silence will be yours however, when the family members, both large and small, slide to the floor unable to reach the seats on the sofas or chairs for the vast quantities of pillows piled high. Think quality not just quantity; consider scale, balance, and proportion limiting yourself to three or four pillows per seven feet of sofa. Never more. Do not try to duplicate the display table at Bergdorf's by piling pretty pillows to the sky.

46 THE HOLIDAY INN EFFECT

If you are a business traveler, you know the feeling of relief when making your way into a hotel room following what feels like a forty-year schlep around the wilderness of life. You exhale deeply and drop your bags at the foot of the bed whispering a prayer of thanks to the gods of mobility who have brought you safely to this nocturnal resting place. As you scan the room your subconscious mind takes inventory, noting the necessities with which your short-term needs will be met: bed, pillows, tables, chair, desk, television, chest of drawers, lamps, various other light sources, a bath with tub, sink, and toilet, and a smattering of towels for drying. And, if you are lucky, you'll spot a minibar just in case the day has been particularly trying. Everything you need to feel at home, right? Wrong! This is everything you need to survive in a modestly civilized manner until the morning when you will don your traveling shoes and venture forth again to slay more dragons, plunder more villages, and scale more castle walls.

But do not kid yourself, Dear Warrior of the Road. You do not find in this environment the nuances that are necessary for you to call this haven for resting "home," unless, like me, you travel with family pictures, scented candles, 25-watt pink lightbulbs, a cashmere throw or two, a few well-loved books, and a leather-bound journal. Yes, home is where the heart is, and our belongings are the signposts we use to navigate the path to our "heart." Our things act as mirrors to our likes, loves, passions, and peccadilloes. In other words, we are the sum total of our stuff.

So Dear Reflective Reader, where's your stuff in your family room? Painfully annoying is the experience of walking in to a room and finding no clue as to the identity of the person whose space I've just entered. Where are your pictures? What books have you read lately and where are the ones you are engrossed in today? Where are the stacks

We are our stuff! Collections, favorite books, and personal photographs are the stuff of life. They reflect who we are, where we've been, and things that interest us. Don't be shy. Share this information with family and friends—on tables, bookshelves, and the walls of your home—you are the star of the show. Gather collections in one area or on one table-top surface, and group photographs on one wall.

of your favorite magazines, cookbooks from which you glean your best dishes, and photo albums filled with memories? Where are your collectables, the things large and small that tell us more about you—the Matchbox cars your mother saved from your childhood or your "Dolls of the World" collection? If the eyes are the window to the soul, then the objects that you surround yourself with provide the framework on which a rich, full life is built. Stop hiding who you are and put it out there for the world to see and love.

47 WHEN BAD TECH HAPPENS TO GOOD PEOPLE

Cables, cords, remotes, and relays; screens, machines, printers, and scanners; gadgets and gizmos, and stations, and more are a family room disaster when piled on the floor. In the midst of today's unmanned tech invasion, our family rooms appear to carry the brunt of the visual disaster; in a nanosecond the mess and the mayhem can spin out-of-control. The tables and floor look like a wasting battlefield whose troops have retreated leaving the weak and injured behind. It's not pretty and it certainly isn't beautiful.

I don't expect you to live without these tools of technology—that would not be practical. I do expect you to gain control of their existence so they don't control you. Let's start with the remotes. At any given moment, no less than six can be found in most family rooms. Many have long since been separated from their purpose in life, serve the same function of others, and just take up space. If you have the tech-savvy that I possess, you may just now be dialing your local techno-trouper firm to consolidate these many into one. More power to you.

After managing your controls, move forward with a cord-cleanse. It's simple really. Scan the room like Vasco da Gama viewing the western horizon and, when you spot a cord, brazenly strewn across the floor, over a table, down the face of a bookcase, or across the seat of your favorite chair, it's time to spring into

purging action and make it disappear. Visit My Personal Favorites Resource Center at www.101ThingsIHateAboutYourHouse.com where we offer a variety of tools for taming the terror of the cords. Pick a product or two, role up your sleeves, and make your family room a bit more beautiful.

48 INADEQUATE TOY STORAGE

Whether your tots have two legs or four, it is a given that they will have copious amounts of toys with which to entertain themselves. Do not panic, this is normal—not always desirable, but certainly normal. Many things happen at the moment of homosapien birth. There's all that pain and mess, screaming and crying, laughter, and, of course, joy. A mental shift occurs that empowers parents to focus solely on the little bundle of joy at the expense of everything or everyone else in the world. It is as nature wants it; this myopic life view for the next few months will decide if that little bundle of joy will turn out to the a Nobel Peace Prize–winner or a serial murderer. So parents, please be myopic. This is your chance to get it right; and part of getting it right is planning so you have the best chance for success.

One of the most important things to plan is where you are going to store the mountains of paraphernalia required to keep your little one engaged and away from power outlets, large machinery, and chemical storehouses. The room of family is a logical destination for all this stuff so let's anticipate storage needs before they press upon us in an unsightly manner. Easy storage solutions include boxes, baskets, and hampers of all shapes and sizes. Built-ins are great if you've thought that far ahead, Dear Makers of Babies. Ottomans with hinged tops can quickly become your best friends as suitable hiding spaces. Train the little one, as you will train yourself, to keep the room tidy by utilizing these storage options. The family room will benefit as will your sanity.

49   FOOD IN THE FAMILY ROOM

Parents make the rules. And parents, shame on you if you don't enforce the rules you make. If you mean "no food in the family room" then plan on standing by your word; otherwise have a plan in place to manage your family's behavior. Food only on trays? Food only on the coffee table? You decide, then you enforce. Anything less will lead to chaos.

Blessed (or cursed) as we are with vast open spaces of "great rooms" and "open floor plans," the tendency for food to find its way into these our primary living spaces seems inevitable.

When you can stand at the refrigerator door and not miss a moment of action on the big screen, chances are that whatever nibble you are noshing will, in part or in full, return to the sofa with you. Like the laws of physics, you can knock your head against a brick wall (literally) trying to fight the cold, hard truth or you can get on the wagon and learn how to steer this wild ride. Parents remember, until Junior writes a check that pays off the mortgage, the roof under which he or she roams is yours. As the homeowner (and parent) you have certain rights of ownership that you should get off your royal behind and enforce (or, in some instances enact). Having conceded to defeat of the no-eating-in the-family-room-battle, your next best strategy is damage control. This is most easily accomplished by the introduction of "trays" into the family's rulebook. The guideline reads something like this: "When food or drink is brought into the family room the use of a tray is required. Family members will lay out a place setting on the tray (just like they would at the dining table). This will include a place mat, plate, napkin, flatware, and drink glass to create as civilized a meal as possible." The trays in question may take many forms from individual serving trays stored in the kitchen or pantry to folding trays on stands that are always returned to their storage closet or cupboard when not in use. Sorry kittens but effort is required even when dining with your TV.

50 PRECIOUS ITEMS IN THE FAMILY ROOM

The 2009 film drama *Precious* garnered six Academy Award nominations and won for best supporting actress, Mo'Nique, and adapted screenplay for writer Geoffrey Fletcher. The film also recalibrated our definition of dysfunction and reminded us all that, when considering our homes, cleanliness is much closer to godliness than the alternatives. How thankful we were that this brave young woman shared her story with us and that good might just have a hand up on all the evil in the world. Praise be!

So what on earth does that have to do with our familial core? Directly very little, actually nothing, except maybe the observation that the family room ain't the place for anything precious. Be it "objects of great financial investment" or "irreplaceable items of sentimental value" both are wrong for this room of the house. Guaranteed, with a blindfold on and my hands tied behind my back, your precious item will be on the short end of the first Nerf-ball pass leaving your precious item and your nerves shattered. So pack the financially precious items away until the kids are less likely to chuck a ball or flip a Frisbee across the room. As for the emotionally precious items (kids christening boots, bearskin rug pictures, and baby's lock of hair, well, you get the picture) spare your teenagers the social cold shoulders guaranteed by the display of such items when "the gang" comes to hang out. Relegate these to your bedroom, office, or walk-in closet instead. The savings to you in psychoanalyst's bills alone will be notable and your enhanced relationship with your offspring will be priceless.

51 ARTLESS WALLS

Like dark windows staring down from skyscraping heights, bare walls in a family room are just scary. Who lives in these rooms? What passions drive them? What loves motivate them? What fears dominate them? What sad excuse for a poster did they pick up at a tag sale and never have properly framed? Once we get past the whole "support the roof and adjoining wall" thing, walls exist as opportunities for self-expression. Art, in its many forms and fashions, offers tools for this expressive exercise. The absence of art, unless you have a proven track record as a collector and pro-test loudly that "you've just not found the right piece," speaks of either fear or laziness. Fear can be managed. Laziness is just un-attractive. If you identify with lazy, you should hand your credit card to a trusted, stylish art-consultant friend (or hired profes-sional) with instructions to "fill it to the brim" and be done with it. Art will arrive and wee decorating fairies will hang your newly purchased collection to the general applause of all in your circle of influence.

THE ART OF CHOOSING ART

If hiring a professional is out of your budgetary league, this three-step guide will be worth your attention:

EDUCATE YOURSELF. I don't care if you don't know Picasso from Pinocchio, now is the time to learn what you like. The art world is vast and the Internet is a huge resource for looking. Scan through a few hundred pieces of art (new, old, and everything in between) and identify the type of art you enjoy. Abstract, figurative, landscape, or portature. These are but a few broad categories into which art is divided.

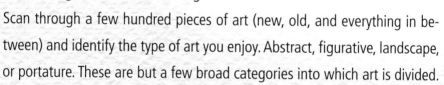

NARROW THINGS DOWN. When you know you like landscapes then busy yourself on eBay or craigslist learning what is currently available and what prices you will pay for a newly found favorite. Your budget may permit an obscure original or a high-ticket masterpiece. Only you can know for sure.

BUY WHAT YOU LOVE. Don't ever buy to match a piece of furniture (decorating gods forbid) but always buy (even if it's poster art) what you can't live without.

I CANNOT OVEREMPHSIZE the importance of a functional family room for the comfort and enjoyment of family and friends. Don't negotiate on these family room musts:

- Comfortable seating. Every seat in the room be it sofa, sectional, club chair, or lounge needs to tip the scale of comfort while remaining true to the classic forms of upholstery. Anything resembling a marshmallow should be avoided like the plague.
- Furniture with cup holders should be taken out and burned. Sorry, but these devises can slip under the radar for pickup trucks, stadium seating, and the occasional home theater. But beyond these isolated uses just because you can, doesn't mean you should!
- Manage your remotes before they control you.
- Carpet or area rugs should cover the floor providing a thick, comfortable experience for walking, lounging, or rolling around like children.
- Make everything user-friendly. The family room is not the place for family heirlooms, costly treasures, or investment quality artwork. If you won't cringe when a Nerf football flies across the room then you know you've got the product selection right.

For more information on the products and resources used in this room, make sure to check out our website at www.101ThingsI HateAboutYourHouse.com.

7

Library

LOST FOREVER ARE MANY of the great libraries of antiquity. These vast collections documented entire civilizations. We are left to surmise their content given their destruction by invading warriors, fire, natural disasters, or the absence of the Dewey decimal system.

One can but imagine strolling along the stone halls of Alexandria's fabled literary cache, admiring the expansive collection of the ancient world's greatest minds. That is, until Julius Caesar's battle plan went sideways leaving his fleet of sailing ships aflame in the bay. Fire quickly jumped ship, incinerating the docks and the adjacent library. Possibly one of histories greatest causalities of war: the loss of this monumental repository wiped from the face of the earth over three centuries of social, political, and historical writings. We're left to guess at the breadth of its content but, rest assured, the loss fuels the consciousness of librarians everywhere. Just try smoking in a public library today. You won't stand a chance.

Threat of incineration aside, libraries maintain important positions within communities today but have little to do with the stacks of books collecting dust in your guest bedroom closet. The idea of a thoughtful gathering of books neatly organized and beautifully displayed can fail to tip the defining scales in our minds. We resolve to think only in terms of stacks of dust collectors and rarely perceive the treasure trove right under our very noses. To this decorator's way of thinking a personal library (electronic reading devices aside) starts with a simple stack of cherished tomes.

52 A POORLY PLACED LIBRARY

Like a lost puppy following its nose in search of home, so, too, is the search for the sacred repository of the soul otherwise known as a library. Now in case the word library, with even larger connotations, scares the bejesus out of you, let me reframe the concept and bring it closer to home for us mere mortals. For library you may wish to substitute "bookshelf in the corner of the family room," "pile of romantic novels teetering on the bedside table," or, my personal favorite, "fourteen issues of the defunct *Metropolitan Home* and half the self-help books from Barnes & Noble balancing precariously on the floor next to the toilet in the bathroom." By making this switch, Dear Thoughtful Reader, any accumulation of bound reading material (supermarket tabloids or whatever your particular periodical poisoning will be excluded from this discussion) holds the promise and prospect of a library.

I find it maddening when the home library is dismissed as impractical or irrelevant. If you own books, their display can be a feature to be admired and enjoyed. That said, certain ideas are worth exploring, not the least of which is how the location of said library speaks volumes for your perceived value of books. If your stacks of tomes rely on the soundness of American Standard to prevent a literary avalanche, then you may wish to rethink the status of books in your home and elect a slightly more visible and certainly more honored place of display. If a designated room is not to be found, craft your library with matching bookcases, in an entry hall, dining room, or corner of the living room. Never fear co-opting prime real estate for the display and enjoyment of your books. It's always a great use of space.

Whether on the floor of your bathroom, next to the bed, or under the coffee table, chances are there is at least one lonely stack of books to be found in your house today. It's time to grow up and find a shelf for their proper storage, display, and use.

53 A Library with Limited Space

As you are selecting the space for a library within your home, don't be stingy with the allocation of space. Generosity of spirit adds to the luxury inherent in books. Thus, it seems reasonable that this gravitas might warrant both an ample and exceptional place within the home. Free yourself from timidity and boldly place books that ignite your passions and curiosities in plain sight. How much space to commit depends on how much of both passion and curiosity you possess. Delicious is the thought of a wood-paneled room tipped to the top with shelves bursting with leather-bound classics. Of equal import is the painted plywood cabinet, neatly displayed near a favorite reading chair, cradling the ten, twenty, or thirty books that captivate you and yours. Do not allow volume to determine location in your home, but rather allow the love for the volumes to inform this decision.

54 DISORGANIZED BOOKS

Dear Skimmer of Matter, it is quite true that Murphy can be a bitch and this is never more true than when you, while in midsentence, decide that the life of your guest, pinned precariously to the story you are telling, will be forever changed when you place Such-and-So's master-piece in their hands. Your memory is blindingly clear as to where in the stacks this literary lovely is lodged. However, you stall before the stacks like Helen

Modern life can be nuts, and that's before we get out of bed in the morning. Get a jump on things by creating order where you can. Books won't argue, fight, or resist your organizing efforts. You'll feel great having accomplished something real and can then brace for the uncontrollable madness just around the corner.

Keller before a hot stove when you realize your memory is not worth the paper it's printed on. The frantic search begins as you pillage and plunder knowing with wobbling certainty that any minute now the little gem will jump off the shelf and into your eager hand. Alas, books don't jump, and the object of your intentions has, by now, lost interest or quietly excused herself, recalling an important dental visit to which she must hurry. Nothing elevates the blood pressure quite like the discrepancy between memory and reality. I have three words, Dear Diviner of Details, that will lower the pressure and elevate the pleasure of your life with books. Organize. Organize. Organize. I care not what system you use, but find a system and commit to its strengths and weaknesses (as nothing, alas, is perfect) with the vigor of a small dog obsessing over its new play toy.

LIBRARY LOGISTICS

I find these four components infinitely helpful in making some sense of the tomes in my homes. Take it from me, your books will rest peace- fully and ready to read, with a bit of assistance from you:

LABELS OF LOVE. If you love your books you will identify them as your own. Be it a stamp of ink, a written insert, or, my personal favorite, the hand-held embossing press. Each lets the world know whose home his precious packet of truth and beauty comes from.

THE LIST OF LOVELIES. Love, like good wine, is meant to spill over the glass and touch everything with its warmth and goodness. Let your love for your library compel you to the next logical step—that of creating a memorializing master list. It is helpful to have when corralling errant editions that have gone missing at the hands of well-meaning surrogates and equally helpful if, heaven forbid, anything untoward should happen to your sanguine stacks. Collecting books dampens our recollection of the costs associated with herding them onto our shelves. A simple list cataloging your collection will make a book easy to replace with or without the assistance of "helping hands," "the rock of Gibraltar," or a "very large red umbrella!"

GAGGLES ARE FOR GEESE. And groups of similar subjects make for a perfectly simple organizational system. The subjects are yours. Remember to own them, as you would own a part of your soul, and then set about grouping the facets of your soul by line of thought and subject matter. It narrows the search considerably when you quickly bypass *Novels of Lust* and *Journals of Quantum Theory,* dashing directly to the *Guides of Travel,* and more specifically, *Walking Tours in Ancient Mesopotamia.* Your good intentions will have shifted the powers of good in the world directly toward the hands of a most anticipatory friend or guest with nary a furrowed brow or chipped nail.

A THROUGH Z. For those with nothing to do all day but sip hot tea and shuffle titles round the room, I recommend alphabetizing the whole lot.

It offers hours of entertainment and a bonding experience with your library equal to none. And when you are done swing by my place. I'll pour the tea and leave you to it, with my deepest appreciation.

55   ## THREADING A NEEDLE IN THE DARK

Good for you. You've found your needle. Haystack be damned! Not much chance of utilizing that needle for anything productive if you can't see your way to a threading experience. Where there

are books, there must be light. Not a blinding spotlight, but a soft pool of warm light (a 75-watt bulb on a dimmer is a good starting point) emanating from a beautifully shaded lamp, atop a table of easy height, next to a deeply upholstered chair; the sum of which quietly insists that you sit and read for awhile. Pink is the color of the stretched-silk lining on the lampshade and a dimmer is deftly placed on the lamp cord. Tea is steeping, and the world can just wait while you enjoy a moment or ten of well-illuminated wonder.

Never discount the knock-out punch books deliver when beautifully displayed. As a background device in any room of the house, books add warmth and instant style. Arrange by size or subject, in vertically stacked runs, or mix it up with horizontal piles; but please, never organize by color. This is reserved for obsessively compulsive photo stylists.

56 PLAIN AS A MUD FENCE

Let us not for a moment, Dear Makers of Magic, forget the strong visual notes struck by books in the landscape of our interiors. Be they gold-embossed first editions or paper-bound marvels you picked up in an airport that fill your shelves, do not discount the impact your library has in decorating the interior of your home. A room void of books reads like blank-lining paper, while a room filled with the magic and wonder of collected treasures takes on the florid magic realized in the finest papers of Venetian bookbinders. So don't hesitate to celebrate the volumes of your life in any room the decorating gods have blessed with extra space.

57 NO PLACE TO WRITE

All the books in the world and all the pools of warm light will matter little if books never leave their shelves and inspire new thoughts or fantastic voyages of the imagination. How wonderful if you have space in your library for a writing table. Indulge this luxury, and snap up a desk or table you love with a comfortable chair thereby elevating the space from ordinary to extraordinary. Far better to have nurtured the creative impulse than to lose the war before the battle's begun. Regardless of your means, a comfortable chair and a clean writing surface is all that is required for creativity to exceed its boarders giving birth to new, colorful ideas.

Quaint, yes. Old fashioned, possibly. But a writing desk seems a perfect complement to the books in our life. It takes up a minimal amount of space and delivers function, beauty, and a level of personal charm. Fit your writing desk with a stylish table lamp, favorite framed photos, and personalized note cards. Now that's beautiful.

SO SHOOT ME BECAUSE THE WALL OF BOOKS is out of frame, but be certain to take a good look at this corner of literary delight. Home to bookcases that match the walnut paneling, this gentlemen's library shares space with a charming grog tray for drinks and allows for some serious cigar smoking thanks to the customized ventilation system installed just for this purpose. Two comfortable chairs, easy lighting, gorgeous layered curtains, and an antique Ziegler rug combine to form a haven for reading, sipping, and puffing to your heart's content. See you after dinner!

To learn more about the other products used in this library of delights log on to My Personal Favorites Resource Center at www.101ThingsIHateAboutYourHouse.com.

8

Guest Bedroom and Bath

"Guests Are Like Fish . . ."

THERE ARE CERTAIN REALITIES IN LIFE that require levelheaded acceptance and fortified preparation. Death, taxes, and houseguests round off the top of my list. With the first, there can be (pray to all the gods) a long lead up to a sudden finality (my preference) that is neither negotiable nor transferable. Taxes, like cockroaches and certain pop songstresses, never actually go away; the anticipation of their next apparition simply fuels sleepless nights. With houseguests, you have the inverse of death—with great suddenness you are inflicted and then rendered slave to a lingering eternity (hell?) of invectives parading through your home in the guise of social pleasantries. Benjamin Franklin once said, "Guests, like fish, begin to smell after three days."

To be certain, the concept of overnight guests is an honor that splits both ways. As host, you have extended hospitality that implies the care and protection of a soul or souls while they are under your roof. Pride, education, and a modicum of good upbringing demand that you fly the colors high making an impression sure to be the talk of your intimates and thus the envy of all. As a guest, your role carries equal import and should be surmounted with all the social charms in your arsenal and tempered with the essence of brevity: your performance should be "of a lifetime," and by so doing rightfully honor your host and all their peculiar eccentricities. Good actors will tell you to "always leave them wanting more" and a wise houseguest will hear these words with diligence and thus always be invited back.

As a host, have you hit the ball out of the park or failed miserably? Don't kid yourself, word spreads quickly. Ensure the reviews from your guests will put you in the best light possible by following our Perfect Hosting Guidelines at www.101ThingsIHateAbout YourHouse.com.

58 A PAIN IN THE NECK

Planes, trains, and taxis, all of various conditions, are common fare for the world-weary traveler. One braces oneself and, if experienced in the art of survival travel, knows how to make the best of whatever the gods of mobility hurl in your direction. Few things offer such promise as that of the pallet for sleeping: the bed, and the icing on the cake of repose, onto which our battered and buffeted head will rest—our pillow. All else can wait, for in this moment our single purpose is reduced to that of horizontal entrenchment. Wild horses, Ritalin-starved children, nor the promise of your host's latest horticultural victory will keep you from just a moment, or ten, of power napping. Then, the unthinkable happens. Rather than the airy loft of a perfectly proportioned down and feather combination your head is rebuffed by a cinderblock's cousin—the compressed foam pillow. All hope is now lost.

Dear Warden of the Weary, take note and act accordingly. As unique as are the prints on our fingers so, too, are our perceptions of comfort when considering a pillow for sleep. Some find noteworthy the attributes of granite when contemplating on what to rest their head. Others dream the dreams of princes only on the loftiest of eiderdown clouds and for every sleepyhead in between there is a preference, oh-so personal. In an artful attempt to cover all bases, cradle all heads, and bring peace to the hinterlands the hotelier's recommendation is simple and to the point. Much as St. Patrick had wisely worked the concept of a three-leaf clover, so, too, will your chamber of hospitality draw divine benefit from the divisor of three. Cover the spectrum from soft to hard and allow your guests to mix, mingle, or manhandle a level of firmness all their own. I prefer placing medium-firm pillows on the bed encased in a protective liner and freshly pressed case. Pairs of softer and firmer pillows in liners and cases are then stacked on a high shelf in a closet just steps away. Your guests will love you in the morning.

59   TOO MUCH OF A GOOD THING (REPRISE)

As noted earlier and as observed in all manner of human experience: there really is such a thing as "too much." Placing one pair of sleeping pillows, of a particular firmness, on a bed and backing up this selection with options, both softer and harder, all neatly stacked on the top shelf of the suite's closet is one thing. A completely new conversation ensues, however, when decorative pillows are mistaken for treasures and thus are stored up against some future day of reckoning. To whom do we address our protest for

inciting the masses to amass such quantities of cushions, bolsters, neck rolls, and such? Enough! Step away from the pillows. If you possess more cushions than the lap of a good reading chair can naturally hold then you've been sold a bill of goods. It doesn't matter if the pillows are pretty, too many is too many. Consider for a moment the stress heaped on your guest when, in the morning, they must make sense of this puzzle of poufs and return them to their original, if questionable, positions. Lacking a map and numbered guide even the most stouthearted will recoil in grief, preferring to avoid the issue completely by tossing themselves (regrettably not your pillows) out the uppermost window.

.60 MISSED OPPORTUNITIES

The onus, thus far, has been on our happy host to artfully anticipate and exquisitely fulfill a guest's needs. The weight of hospitality is not for sissies, Dear Receiver of Kindness, so buck up and take note. With the lofty issue of pillows behind us, let's submerge ourselves in the sublimities of practicality. Rest, for a moment, your firmly toned tush on one side of the bed or the other; allow for a second your mind to wander to the farthest corners of the world, and now bring yourself back to this pleasant but unfamiliar scene.

If you think being a guest is a challenge, try being a host. Anticipation is the key to successful hosting. What might your guests need to make their stay exceed expectations? How might you prepare to ease their stress when far from home? Put yourself in their traveling shoes and make your hosting list. A little effort pays big dividends. Now that's beautiful!

Yes, pretend you are a guest in your own home. You've stirred from your sleep of the dead, sat bolt upright in bed, fought back the split-second panic of not knowing where-in-the-world you are, and have begun a nocturnal list of certain basic needs:

No. 1: what is the time? No. 2: has it been days or weeks since water last passed through your parched lips? No. 3: regardless of the answer to No. 2, your body is sharply suggesting that relief is required and thus either a bedpan or an en suite bath should be urgently required. No. 4: though you vaguely recall arriving with a piece or two of luggage, finding something in bags you don't completely remember and whose present location could be Cairo or downstairs in the entry hall, you pray for a dressing gown as you grope the end of the bed for a throw or a loose bedsheet. No. 5: with body wrapped, relieved, and rehydrated the plight of the jet-lagged can make its presence known.

Interesting, current books and a small DVD collection with the required viewing equipment can be a lifesaver in the wee hours of the morning when sleep is as close as the northern-most pole. Do you know your guest well? Then customize their reading and viewing options in a manner that reveals your thoughtfulness and the depth of your friendship. Perfect strangers visiting on the behest of a mutual friend? Go for things upbeat in tone and middle of the road in subject matter leaving scorching religious or political diatribes or movies involving bodily dismemberment far from view.

Reality can be rough, so put yourself through the paces before you welcome a guest. The obvious, like clean, empty drawers scented by lavender sachets and wide, open closet space with ample wooden hangers are good first steps in the finest care of guests. By tapping a heavy dose of empathy, you can offer soothing calm to even the most tormented travelers.

61 BARE NAKED WINDOWS

By no means limited to the rooms of hospitality, there is no time like the present to review and adjust our thinking and execution when it comes to the draping of fabrics on and around windows. Earlier we spoke about addressing windows, now is our opportunity to decipher how we best strike balance between the decorative and the functional. Kids be damned and spouses may suffer in silence, but guests in our home should not be forced to suffer our follies or fancies at the expense of a good night's sleep.

Our primary objective when pondering the dressing of windows in your guest room, regardless of your belief on the subject or of the balance in your bank account, is that of light control. If the issue of blocking out light is key, be it of solar type or the mercury-vapor type often used in street lamps, then the response should be direct and win applause on all accounts. The most rudimentary of

roller blinds is a place to start. This tried and true option is both functional and economical. Variations on this theme are endless, and as your budget allows I encourage you toward flights of fancy. But as you take wing remember the basic objective. As the basic is being remembered give thought to these convergences: Is light best controlled by mounting the shade inside the frame of the window or out? At the same time, ruminate over how the window is framed and what mounting method best underscores this truth.

Beautiful drapery, like fine couture, creates gentle awareness rather than the forced acknowledgment demanded by less subtle devices. When considering these artful additions, do so with my valuable guidance lest your windows look like a cheap suit at a funeral. Here are three tips to top your list of curtain consideration:

- Take 'em to the top. Creating a tall, elegant line from floor to ceiling is the objective with curtains in any room. Place the rod as close to the ceiling or molding as possible. Doing otherwise leaves you with a visually truncated experience and awkwardness for all.

- To line or not to line. All curtain fabric looks best when lined with cream or white cotton and when viewed from the street to offer a consistency from window to window. Cost can be a factor. I would pursue a simple curtain fabric to offset the cost of lining, so important to the finished product is this dressmaker's touch.

- Never puddle. Like shoulder pads and Lycra leggings, puddle curtains are fashion items just looking for new victims. Curtains should "break" (like a gentleman's trousers) one-half inch from the finished floor. No more and no less. Period. End of discussion. For more ideas on curtain design and installation advice, visit My Personal Favorites Resource Center at www.101ThingsIHateAboutYourHouse.com.

There are fully acceptable variations to fine drapery, as there is prêt-á-porter in the fashion world. The key to success in this area is clarity regarding your desires and an understanding of what is being procured. If hand-stitching, lining and interlining, and

Naked windows are decorating death, and coverings don't come cheap. Establish a budget, determine the window covering of your dreams, and set about making your dreams come true.

custom-dyed passementeries are desired then please be prepared to pay for your piper and enjoy the resulting music for years to come.

If these symphonic tunes are enticing but your budget pleads for a good cassette deck, then make that cassette deck your own and secure the best sound quality possible. Numerous sources (national as well as local) are available for panels of unlined fabric ready for mounting on poles or rods, then artfully suspended at your window. Remember, take your rods as high as your architecture allows (yes, tucked up against crown molding) to allow for the greatest drop of fabric possible. This illusion supports the scale of most rooms where height is typically scarce.

62   UNIMAGINATIVE SMALL SPACES

However hospitable your heart may be, limitations presented by the laws of physics can be a bitch. Do not despair, but instead be inspired by a goal and be creative in realizing your version of success. When space is limited, the idea of a writing desk seems preposterous, much as does the thought of a reading chair. Is your spatially challenged room such that a choice must be made? Maybe the reality of your real estate is such that both are but a dream. So be it. How might a creative mind rise to the occasion while still offering guests the benefits of these two idyllic services? I'm seeing a lovely lap desk and an attractively

upholstered "lounging pillow" (oh, you remember this from junior high school: a cushy chairback with arms you recline on, while lounging on your bed and talking on the phone for hours! Turns out that in a smart, snappy fabric this comfy cushion is terribly practical! Who knew? And when not in use, it can join the cast of alternate pillows on the shelf in the guest closet) with which to prop up an otherwise horizontally bound scholar. Use your imagination and then bask in the warmth of your own success.

63 A Stingy Stocking of Supplies

Whether through the absence of sense or abduction by surly, dutiful TSA agents, a traveler's lack of certain personal necessities is all too common these days and allows a forward-thinking host yet another venue for display of wizardly powers of foreknowledge. A bathroom cabinet stocked with wide ranges of hygiene supplies can vanquish the stink right off a frazzled guest. So over the years condition yourself to collect samples of soaps, lotions, scrubs, and creams; brushes, flosses, pastes, and masks; aspirins, analgesics, antihistamines, and rubs; cologne, perfumes, waters, and washes. Shoe horns and shine kits, needles with threads, and a hairdryer or two can ease the finger from most any panic button. As your space allows, serve up an iron with board and a variety of spray starches. Your thoughtful gathering of this-and-thats will lift you into the pantheon of hosts and actually cost you little, if you're smart about the whole thing. Just think of all the random gift and sample bag fodder for which you now have solid practical use.

Much about design and decorating comes with a price tag, depressing as it is. But I'm happy to report that stocking your guest bed and bath can be almost free if you play your cards right. Frequenting charity events, department store sample counters, and upscale hotel suites can be a boon to your hosting budget. If only a new sofa were so free and easy.

64 AN UNAPPRECIATIVE GUEST

Now, Dear Glamorous Guest, 'tis parody time in the land of travel. As the auger of honor swings both ways, now is the time to take note with care. Commandments are commanded for reasons that, at times, mere mortals miss. Not for lack of earnest, or for lack of wit, but often for lack of consciousness. Open your eyes, place yourself squarely in your host's fabulous shoes, and heed these Lodging Commandments:

Thou shall not arrive unannounced. *Ever.*

Thou shall not stay for more than three days. While you may scoff at this concept it is a simple and tried fact that guests, regardless of their intimacy with their host, go stale after three days. Guard against this natural phenomenon of overstaying your welcome as you would against the loss of other perishables and be certain of being invited back.

Thou shall not assume inclusion in household events (meals, parties, excursions, etc.). If you are invited then graciously participate with energy and excitement, all of which reflect favorably on your host.

Thou shall not open a closed door. *Ever.* When you are shown to your room, you have tacitly been given the lay of your land while in residence. Respect for these parameters can save your neck as any Twihard will tell you.

Thou shall not sit idly by while your host waits on you hand and foot. Assert yourself in clearing dishes, walking the dog, or loading the dishwasher. If beaten back by a mindful host, graciously acquiesce and entertain others with a witty story or engaging conversation.

Thou shall not presume the availability of local transportation by your host or their family members. Rent a car, download a bus schedule, or secure a local cab company's phone number without asking for use of the yellow pages. Be self-sufficient at all times.

Thou shall not venture, uninvited, into the kitchen for late night foraging. Unless offered free rein by your host never consider the kitchen, the bar, or the root cellar to be yours for the taking. Better, by far, to stock up on PowerBars and fifths of scotch than to force the discomfort of banishment by an egregious breach of conduct.

Thou shall not be a cheapskate. If there is staff in the house (a housekeeper, for instance, who has assisted your stay) leave a thank-you note on your bedside table with a gratuity for their services. Your visit has expanded their responsibilities and, while confident in your host's overtime compensation policies, never let it be said that you did not acknowledge the staff's efforts on your behalf. If drinks or dinner out become an option during your visit then quietly leave the table during dinner and surreptitiously supply the establishment with your credit card along with clear instructions for presenting the preprocessed bill. This quiet gesture exemplifies your generous heart trussed up in all that Gucci and Prada and is the least you can do in acknowledging your host's gracious hospitality.

Thou shall not neglect sending a thank-you card. No doubt, flowers, wine, a treasured book, or any number of other gifts are appropriate at this moment and will be appreciated to the same degree that care was taken at their selection. Gift or no gift, you must never not send a thank-you card. It's simply bad manners and makes you look like a bum from the sticks regardless of the labels on your luggage.

Thou shall not fail to extend the same hospitality. Turn about is always fair play. So when considering the pros and cons of lodging with friends, be certain you are prepared to extend yourself in like manner. This is known as the "comes-around" part of the equation.

65 A Communication Breakdown

Even the most generous hosts at times are thwarted by the limitations of space. No amount of wishing or praying will add a guest bedroom and bath to your current square footage so alternate plans must be in place should you decide to extend the laurel branch of hospitality. Once the invitation has been issued, there is no turning back. Be clear with your intended guest what it is you are offering. A foldout sofa in the living room is perfectly acceptable but should not be sprung on a weary traveler upon their arrival. News of a shared bath should be treated the same. Manage your guest's expectations as well as your own, and everyone will enjoy the experience.

A generous heart is to be admired, but balance generosity with realism. If you've got space for guests, your kindness will shine in your invitation. You court disaster when you overreach no matter how good it feels in the moment. Offering more than you have to deliver might just find you sleeping in your own bathtub. And that's not beautiful!

MY TWO CENTS ON TIGHT-QUARTERS HOSTING

Here's a short list of ideas for a space-pinched host to make your hospitality as big as the outdoors:

PLAN AHEAD. Have bed linens (sheets, blankets, pillows, etc.) at hand and ready for use. Stack them carefully in a closet or on a nearby table, and do it in a manner that communicates your preparedness. Nothing is worse than a tired guest's downward spiral playing out behind you while you rummage through closet and cabinets looking for an extra set of pillowcases.

SET A SCHEDULE. Because a lot of sharing will occur, set clear guidelines that allow both you and your guests to navigate daytime and evening necessities. Everything from bathroom to television to coffee maker can find its way onto a well thought out schedule, allowing you to get to work on time while affording your guest both access and ease.

COMMUNICATE CLEARLY. State your truth without hesitation or apology so your guest understands perfectly the marks to be hit for a successful run of show. "I must leave the house by 8 AM to catch my train so I'll use the bathroom from 7:15 until 8:00 tomorrow morning. After that, it's all yours." Supplementing a well-defined schedule, this type of clear, verbal communication prevents misunderstandings and works to the benefit of both parties.

Here's a look at a charming guest chamber realized for clients and illustrating the simple nature of a beautiful room. Curtains artfully crafted: check. Antique bed, comfortably covered with a tailored spread: check. Writing desk doing double duty as a bedside table (a great trick in a tight space): check. Practical side chair for desk and dressing use: check. Tasteful art pleasantly hung: check. Softly shaded lamps casting pleasant light: check. Don't know about you, but I'd unpack my suitcase in this room any day or night.

To learn more about the other perfect products to create beautiful and comfortable guest bedrooms and baths log onto www.101ThingsIHateAboutYourHouse.com.

9

Children's Bedroom and Bath

Little Bodies, Big Needs

ONCE LONG AGO when considering our society's offspring, an author spun rhymes describing the essential elements that make up our youngsters. "Sugar and spice and everything nice" topped the list for the little ladies in our midst. Acknowledging the ruff and tumbles of our male counterparts, our poet lists their makeup as including "frogs and snails and puppy-dog tails." "Designer handbags and belly rings" might sum up things for today's young ladies while "Transformers and Nintendo DSs" draw attention to the young men of our acquaintance. This is not a judgment but simply an observation that our world has changed and so, too, has the Mini Me in our lives.

The very nature of change, that catalyst upon which civilizations have crumbled, delivers fairly good odds that what has worked in the past for our young ones might be in need of some adjustment today. Not that fairy princesses don't still need castles; and never question the requirements of cowboy for a herd or two. But let's face it, today's princesses and cowboys have evolved just a bit. Seems that today young princesses get along just fine with or without their knight in shining armor, and in similar stereotype-blurring fashion, junior cowboys can whip up a gourmet barbeque, decorate a tent, and sew a new hem in their buckskin chaps without impingement on their manhood. Chances are we, as the adults in the room, might want to rethink bits and pieces of our assumptions regarding the rooms in which they'll sleep and play.

66 An Obnoxiously Themed Room

Rarely has a song and its associated images so successfully been seared into our psyche as during the terrifying trip through this seemingly inoffensively parked slice of amusement called the *It's a Small World After All* ride. All those multinational faces beaming so brilliantly in our general direction, a color spectrum that proves entirely possible the idea that one could go the rest of one's life and never see a shade of pastel again, ever.

Now Dear Pupil of Prepubescence, imagine if you will the long-term damage inflicted when themes, however charming, are used to frame our little tadpoles' environs. Just as revenge is best served cold, so novelty is best offered up in small manageable doses. Walk the thin line, balance precariously on the precipice if you must, but rein in the impulse to swaddle your starry-eyed little ones in thematic sheeting, branded carpeting, and corporately licensed wall coverings. Not only will your increasingly sane child grow to thank you (in complete, nonjargonized sentences), but your pocketbook will blow kisses of contentment in your direction.

For who could bear the sight of gangling, young teens disallowing their friends' entrance to their room for fear of the social leprosy certain to consume their young personage, should their peers ever get an eyeful of their Speed Racer retreat or overblown Barbie boudoir?

Spare yourself and your teens by opting for fun, youthful backgrounds that will grow with your children and not box them in. Fill the walls with pinup boards, blackboards, and the

If you can't live without some thematic display in your tiny tot's room, then opt for the 10-40-50 approach to decorating your child's room. That breaks down to 10 percent for thematic material of your choosing, 40 percent for age-specific items and furnishings, and 50 percent for items that will grow with your child (pin-up and black boards, writing desk, overstuffed reading chair, table and floor lamps . . . you get the picture).

occasional dart board or two and let offsprings' blossoming lives be displayed through pictures, invitations, and favorite moments. The furniture should be practical (spend good money on a study desk and chair) and interesting, maybe bordering on funky. It is a kid's room so let fun lead the way, but let it be so lead as to avoid cliché opting instead for chic. Online retailers and local tag sales and auctions are great sources for interesting pieces for tomorrow's movers and shakers.

67 OUTRAGEOUSLY EXPENSIVE KID'S FURNISHINGS

Free passes are given to parents when it comes to their children's pet names. These terms of endearments illicit tacit "ohs" and ahs" from the most balanced among us, adding fuel to the fire and guaranteeing no end to the cycle. Be that as it may, the occasional action of parents that transmutes their terms of tenderness into items of considerable consequence requires my comment. In other words, sometimes parents spend stupid amounts of money on things their children simply don't need and may never fully appreciate. My inclination, Dear Pedantic Parent, is simple—don't. Do not hunt down the cradle from the nursery at the Petit Trianon, for use in Junior's nursery. Do not wrangle your way through European auction houses searching for a seventeenth-century tester bed on which to deposit Missy and her teddy bear collection. Don't insist that New York City's finest antique dealers scour their inventories for a fine Italian writing desk at which to plop down Skippy and his science fair project. Precious objects should not vie for attention in the same room as your family's true treasures.

68 IRRELEVANT ART

Successfully selecting art for children's rooms depends on the selection of art that is relevant to the children in your home. Involving your kids in the selection process of art for their rooms is a great first step for connecting the dots for the child.

Any discussion of hanging art whether in a child's room or in a living room, can be split into two conversations. No. 1: the display. No. 2: the selection.

The theory behind the pleasing display of art remains immutable regardless of the room in the house. Issues of scale, proportion, balance, and symmetry should influence the decisions long before the first bit of plaster is pierced. When in doubt about art on a wall always opt for fewer larger pieces. Three 40-inch square paintings, prints, or panels evenly spaced across a bedroom wall will always look better than fourteen small pieces scattered across the same wall. Keep it simple and keep it sane. This leaves the selection of art on our list of things to do and, rather than shirk my responsibility, it's time we tackle this highbrow topic.

When pondering art for a child's bedroom, consider how much money you have to spend. To say $10 is no less correct than to say $1,000. Your budget may have you mixing Tempera paints and encouraging the inner Picasso in your child and her neighborhood friends or you may find yourself online, or dashing in and out of local galleries and dealers all in search of a piece you can't live without. Your budget should dictate your actions. Hunting in appropriate parts of the jungle and listening to your heart when presented with an option that fits comfortably within your financial expectations makes for a successful art expedition and the pride of ownership. Art brings great joy and satisfaction when its acquisition is handled in a responsible manner.

69 Toyland Run Amok

I've successfully raised a pair of Yorkshire terriers and will be the first to admit that the nurturing of children is a tad bit foreign to me. However, I find no support in all the available literature that says that parents must forgo control of their home because Junior or Princess need to stretch their little play muscles. Cavorting can take place in one specific area of the house without any lingering damage to the wee ones psychological or physiological development. All it takes is a backbone on Mom and Dad's part and the tiniest bit of supportive discipline to see the successful consolidation of play space that was once scattered hither and yon. Dear Dazed Parents, feel free to select where in your comfortable casita this zone of play is most perfectly situated. By the exertion of your will, you can make it so. Select an area convenient to your life, your work, and your play and then start confining the little ones to this, their very own play zone. Your sanity and lifestyle will applaud these efforts, and your kids will love having their own area for fun.

70 FORGETTING A KID'S-EYE VIEW

If it makes me crazy, can you imagine the push-me, pull-you effect some of our most basic design decisions have on the little ones scampering around our houses? No wonder they're such nervous wrecks all the time. Are you perfectly clueless as to what I mean? Then join me on a walking, nay crawling, tour of your house. On your knees, if you please. Isn't it interesting how things change from this point of view? Sure, go wash your hands and brush your teeth. Simple enough instructions until you approach a bathroom Pullman only to find yourself staring at a cabinet door completely unable to reach the faucet, soap, toothbrush holder, or neatly folded hand towel. Attention deficit disorder being what it is, I'm off to chase the dog, having quickly forgotten the task at hand. And, what about navigating the kitchen in a meaningful productive manner? How nice would a bit of self-reliance be (Mom is always after me to do more for myself), and imagine how self-reliant I might be if every bit of food, drink, and service utensil were not hovering above my head in cabinets or pantries. While getting into bed is simple enough— everything in the little tyke's closet hung high only makes for a frustrating beginning or end to anyone's day.

Place age-appropriate items within reach of your children's grasp to aid in their feelings of independence and your rest and relaxation. Purchase step stools for your children's bathrooms (built-in, pull-out models win prizes for the think-ahead parent), install a below-counter pullout-drawer refrigerator for self-help juice and water, and a lower-level microwave can be a great source of personal accomplishment for Junior and his after school snacking.

Put everyday items within reach of your littler half and involve them in making your house a home. Dishes stored in lower drawers or pullout cabinets eliminate the need for parental assistance when it's time to set the table. Set your little one up for success in every room of the house.

71 AGE-INAPPROPRIATE DESIGN

Unless you strive for the personality disorders of Baby Jane Hudson as portrayed by Bette Davis in the 1962 psychological thriller *What Ever Happened to Baby Jane?* the idea of framing your child's life with age-inappropriate design should compel you to ditch the kid crap and stay current with your child's life and the times in which she lives. This is best illustrated by teenagers old enough to drive, who are forced to climb into twin-size bunk beds at the end of their day. Like other rites of passage, I'm a strong believer in a

Mom double bed arriving on or around any young person's

and Dad sixteenth birthday. Your little one ain't so little

it's time to get over any more; and this is a warm, nurturing way

your heel dragging on the to let them know you know they are on

subject of Junior growing up their way to adulthood. Ikea, along

before your very eyes. They will with online retailers and local fur-

grow whether you want them to niture showrooms, is jammed with

or not, so make the best of a ma- stylish options that won't ding

turing problem and match their your pocketbook but can help

chronological age with the furnish- sharpen the design awareness of

ings in their rooms. A teenager (13 your teenager's living space.

and older) should be sleeping in

a double bed, not in a childish

twin. The progression from twin ## 72 WHEN SAFETY IS IGNORED

to double is a rite of passage.

Make it memorable for Okay, Dear Designing Parent, back on

your young lady or your knees; it is time for another lap 'round

gentleman. the house. This time we're all about safety for

the little monsters housed in your stylish abode. Safe-

ty and style go hand in hand, which is something we must never

forget, but forgetting is usually not the problem. As our earlier

tour a-la-mode pointed out, it is really a matter of perspective; our

view typically differs greatly from that of our offspring.

A few highlights from the house tour: bare-naked stair-cases! I cringe and shutter when in a home filled with children and I see a wood staircase devoid of a runner. Having taken a tumble down one my-self, I'm skeptical of no runner when only adults are involved. There is no persuading me otherwise when kids enter the mix. Carpet the stairs and do it now.

While I'm not one to cry out that "the sky is fall-ing!" I do believe a gra-cious home should have safety measures and procedures in place. I'm always speechless when tour-ing a home's second story and I find that there are not safety ladders (rolled and stored discrete-ly in a nearby closet) in each bedroom. Do the kidlets know how to work the security system? And what is the family plan should, gods on high forbid, there be a natural disaster? I find it most reassuring when the children take guests on a brief but well-presented tour of the safety procedures. My cocktail always tastes better knowing there's an eight-year-old in the house who knows what to do in case of earthquake, tornado, or flood.

73 WHEN LIFE CRAMPS OUR STYLE

It seems to me that homes fall into one of two categories: either yours is the house everyone hangs out at or not. There are no brownie points one way or the other, but understanding how your home fits into the burgeoning social life of your children can go a long way toward aligning your decorating dreams with domesticat- ed design. A quick survey of your kingdom should give you a clue as to which category your house falls. If you find yourself texting your children that dinner is ready and they come from points north, east, south, and west, then chances are your home isn't the designated hangout spot in the neighborhood. If, on the other hand, you must count noses in the game room before setting your table for dinner each night then chances are you're the default den parent for your young ones and the marauding masses otherwise known as their friends.

Both camps have their pluses and minuses. We'll save that discussion for another book. However, we must pay a glancing bit of attention to the design and decorating ramifications each brings to the table. On one hand, things are pretty much as they appear. Family of five, dining table seats six. Three teenagers, three double beds, etc. But when you're the de facto event coordinator for your neighbors and their kids, things change exponentially, and you need to get a grip on it all before it gets a grip on you. Extra seating in all family-oriented rooms? Check. Bunk or trundle beds in bedrooms? Check. Easily augmented work and study stations in each child's bedroom? Check. Extra bed and bath linens? Check. And the list goes on, but personally, I wouldn't want it any other way. What fun to experience a house full of kids! It makes the cocktail hour all the more delightful.

Understanding the role your home plays in the social lives of your children allows for some thoughtful and practical decorating. A constant swirl of adolescent energy makes a good case for folding chairs, sectional seating, and expanding tabletops. Don't cramp anyone's style by failing to plan.

Shocking as it may be, there are times when clients want what they want regardless of the words of wisdom not-so-humbly offered. So a themed room it was for this three-year-old boy whose papa played minor league ball! When given a task, this decorator knows how to connect all the dots. So we began with a custom carpet depicting home plate, with a few baselines just for good measure. The dugout, cleverly containing bed and storage, extends the length of the room while a mural of the field of play (complete with the visiting team made up of Junior's favorite animals from the zoo) wraps the three adjoining walls. Even the windows are touched with the sport as we used glove leather to detail the muslin shades. The vintage chair was found in a dealer's attic virtually untouched since 1970: a perfect, if costly, touch for the future heavy hitter.

Ready to chime in with questions or comments? Be my guest by logging onto www.101ThingsIHateAboutYourHouse.com.

10

Master Bedroom and Bath

CREATING A GRACIOUS HOME only has meaning if the foundation, the reason for all the fuss, is out of intensive care and breathing on its own. If you're single then love yourself and let the world know just how fabulous you are by the way you care for No. 1. If you are partnered and thus share the roller coaster ride of home décor with that someone, well bravo for you. Now roll up your sleeves and get to work. Not only do you need to love the heck out of yourself, but also you get to shower endless love and attention on the stranger snoring on the pillow next to yours. It's a magical mix filled with love, hate, and everything in between. If you get it right more than you get it wrong, the payoff is priceless. So take all the help you can get and pay close heed to my advice about decorating the space you retreat to when the world beats the heck out of you—your bedroom. In this context, there is no more important room in the house. Period.

Entertain all you'd like. Dazzle the neighbors, their friends, and their kids—if, at the end of the day, the relationship sheltered in the master suite falters, then none of the other stuff will matter a hill-of-beans. While we're clear that good design will not bring about world peace or stem the spread of hunger or hatred, if attention is paid it will level the playing field and help give your relationship that fighting chance.

74 DECORATING EXCESSES

While encouraging grace and beauty in every corner of the home, I'm particularly insistent on the matter in the master bedroom. This is the private zone, the area to which one retreats to indulge in the most private moments of life. The deepest of sleeps, the quietest of quiets, and the highest of heights; they are all realized here. And yes, you should always have a lock on the door and don't be afraid to use it! Dear Decorating Doubles Partners, here is where a principle bears repeating: run from excess. I can't tell you the master suites I've seen that rely on too much of something for their decorating spine. Excessive use of ruffles, excessive use of lace, excessive mindless clutter, too much testosterone or too much estrogen all upset the harmony in this notoriously challenging space. And decorating gods deliver us from the happy homemaker who decides to spice things up by a master bedroom redo inspired by a Parisian brothel. If you really believe a stripper pole is all that stands

I believe what you do in your bedroom is your business. My business is to make that room look as good as possible while you romp and play to your heart's content. Up go the red flags of caution when the décor conjures up the tasteless tactics of a tacky Vegas cathouse. Keep your playful self out of your bedroom's permanent decorating decisions unless your eyes are on a home-based career change.

between you and a blissful relationship then I've got land in South Florida you really should know about.

Preferable, by far, is a suite of rooms (which in a perfect world would consist of a chamber for sleep, an area for lounging, a bath for two and a closet for each), simply and beautifully furnished. Couples yearning for decorating détente need to determine what end of the hormonal scale the décor of the room will tip. Ladies, I have clients swear by an overtly feminine décor for their shared suites, maintaining that the slight pause all those ruffles give their husbands is just the edge they need. For others, the desire to romp and retire in a decidedly masculine space tips the scales in unexpected ways.

Take note: there is a time and place for everything. Keep items associated with a romantic tryst properly put away. Personally, I think getting ready is half the fun. Our intimate experiences are life's precious moments, not lifestyle or decorating choices. Intimate moments should be treated as such and not permanently splashed around your home as the trappings of a cheap tart—which means the striper pole, lambskin-lined restraints, and trousseau of edible underwear are best stored discreetly rather than spotlighted for the world to see. So guys and gals remember, when planning your bedroom, success is found in a little mystery not the screeching obvious.

75 POORLY PLANNED BEDSIDE TABLES

All the negotiated aesthetics in the world will fade quickly when you are forced to rummage on the floor for your book, eyeglasses, carafe of water, or tissue box. Side tables are vital in any room, but in the master suite, bedside table selection dictates the ease with which you carry out many daily rituals. For some, bedside needs revolve around their mobile phone and a table lamp, while for others the list of nocturnal necessities is ever growing and changing.

One of the joys of decorating is the introduction of asymmetry into a room, whereby matched pairs (in this case bedside tables) are supplanted by related pieces. Guess what, in this scenario each of you gets exactly what you want. For you, the simplest of tables offering a compact horizontal surface perfect for your favorite lamp and your cherished iPhone. No drawers, no storage, no extra surfaces to collect much of anything. Meanwhile, on the other side of your world, your partner has a small village built into the condo-cabinet on his or her side of the bed. Multiple lighting options (from a discrete clip-on book lamp to a portable self-tanning machine), shelf and stacking storage for half the bestsellers on the *New York Times* bestseller's list, baskets for tissues, trays

for medicines, cases for spare reading glasses, a port for a laptop, a small printer, and three types of water (flat, sparkling, and lemon infused) are just the beginnings of what is shoehorned into this maximum storage facility. Decorating disaster—most likely. Happy partner—definitely. There are worse things in the world than a happy (if cluttered) partner.

76 WHEN HI-TECH RULES THE BEDROOM

Form your own opinion please, but the last place I want my laptop, iPad, or Droid is my bedroom. Having retreated from the maddening world, I want to sleep, read (old-fashioned, bound books, please), and make love—and not always in that order.

When it comes to the prima sanctorum, the only good technology is what is locked outside the bedroom door. This is no place for laptops, iPads, or any Internet-connected device. Period. As the days of landlines quickly fade from memory, the bedside placement of a mobile phone device for the purpose of communication with the outside world is a necessary evil and can be tolerated. All other technical devices should simply be banned.

I realize I may have just lost some of my younger readers who, it seems, came into this world with a texting devise in their hands and for whom a disconnected moment seems a torture worse than attending a Josh Groban concert. To those readers I say, "Grow up." If the object of your far-flung, late-night text is that important then maybe someone's in the wrong bed! As a recent convert to all things "social" and "media," believe me, I understand the temptations associated with constant contact and relentless access. But I am also reminded of a lesson learned at my parent's dinner table, in the ancient days prior to voice mail and answering machines. My father was clear on the concept, "Just because the phone rings does not mean we are obliged to answer." As foreign as this may sound to some, I promise there are great rewards to disconnecting. Try it, you'll like it.

77 THE BEDROOM TV

Closely related to the topic of technology, but warranting special comment, the television looms large on the bedroom horizon. With two principle activities in mind (lovemaking and sleeping), all design decisions must support success in these key endeavors. Successful multitasking is a myth; doing one thing well and seeing it through to the end appears, if we believe the research wonks, to be the only way to achieve maximum, sustainable results. Regardless of the bed-centric activity embarked upon, no one wants her beauty sleep compromised or any other activity to achieve less than maximum results. So limit the range of your bedroom activities to a short list made up of only the highly desirables. Sleep, sex, and the occasional perusal of a Pulitzer Prize–winning novel seem the most obvious. Staring at a technologically advanced LED-screen while numbly surfing through 800 cable channels, just doesn't make the cut if you ask me.

78 Hardwoods Under Foot

As we've noted earlier, I'm not particularly fond of bare hardwood floors. While beautiful to look at (yes, many a dreamy magazine spread romanticizes lustrous bare wood floors) the realities of daily life trump even the most aesthetic inclination. Bedrooms should overflow with the softest, warmest, and most comfortable experience under foot. This goes double for the master suite. I even suggest additional padding beneath the area rug or carpet of choice, which will provide a bit more comfort and slightly more privacy.

79 Bringing the Office to Bed

If your professional life demands that you work, go to a desk in your office area somewhere else in the house. If your desk can go nowhere else but in your shared bedroom, then negotiate with your partner a reasonable work schedule. Once these hours have past, turn off the electronic devices and start paying attention to the love of your life. Otherwise, one day you'll look up from your backlit screen only to discover how very alone you are.

Guarding your bedroom from the encroachments of life is not for the weak at heart. If you have room in your house for your office anywhere other than the bedroom, move it there. Real men and women may find their mettle tested when asked to relocate their station for work to another corner of the house. Real men and women also understand the value of a gracious home, one where rewards for good design far outweigh the challenges.

OFFICE-IN-THE-BEDROOM ETIQUETTE

If the house you're in won't make room for an office in another room, then keep in mind these concepts:

KEEP IT SMALL. Focus your attention on occupying as little space as possible while addressing only the most pressing corporate needs. A phone, space on a writing desk for a stylish lamp and your laptop, and a file cabinet fitted into an adjacent closet is an ideal to shoot for.

BECOME A NEAT FREAK. Less painful than it sounds, realize that every mess you leave on your alter of employment will stare you in the face all night long. And unless you're single (and at this rate may be for quite some time), you'll be hard pressed to impress a suitor with piles of daily tasks ruining the moment. Live by the rule that when you close up shop for the day everything is promptly put away. Your relationships deserve this fighting chance.

IF YOU SHARE YOUR BEDROOM with a spouse or partner, be respectful of their needs by posting clear hours of business after which your partner is free to move about the bedroom without fear of being asked to file a letter or fetch fresh coffee.

---

80 Brazen Bed Linens

Fashion seems to make the world go 'round. Bring on the runways, the models, and give us racks of clothes and piles of shoes to rummage through like children on Christmas morn. Color, pattern, and texture abound as we wrap, zip, and button our way into sartorial nirvana. Chances are good that beneath all this colorful magnificence we will find, if it exists at all (!), white- or cream-colored undergear. There may be many reasons for this, but I believe the general inclination is toward a perception of freshness and cleanliness. Few things say clean and fresh with such visceral clarity as does crisp, white cotton; and there is nothing quite as delightful to

slip between as beautiful set of bed linens of the same color. Always get it right by selecting cream or white: pipe, embroider, or trim your selection in any color and fashion you wish, while sleeping with a classic every night of your life. As for the counting of threads, at some point it just gets silly. Look for the long staple, Egyptian cotton with a thread count between 400 and 600 from a reputable linen manufacture and you won't go wrong. Paying more for claims of 1,200-plus counted threads could put you on the short-list for the sale of a certain bridge in Brooklyn.

Whether you are drawn to crisp whites or luxurious cream-colored bed linens or have opted for all the colors of the rainbow, caring for your investment will enhance your enjoyment and prolong its lifespan.

81 CAVERNOUSLY SCALED BATHS

Many people have a tendency to exaggerate the perceived value of the master bath. Yes, we're told that kitchens and baths sell homes, and I believe this can be true. But really, people, this fact does not need to translate into front-loading, disproportionate square footage and decorative flourishes into these spaces. The elaborate baths of Istanbul are both great and in a foreign country for a reason. Let's keep it that way. They exist to house communities of

bathers and to act as a hub for the neighborhood's social life. This is not the case with your privy—so back off the vast expanses of stone, tile, and gilded lilies. Consider, if you will, a master bath appropriate to your needs rather than one in direct competition with the spa at the Ritz Paris. You will enjoy your daily rituals more, and your friends will have one less thing to laugh about behind your back.

For every homeowner there are specific priorities for master baths, but for those who desire the deluxe type, I recommend: twin Pullmans, heated stone floors, two-person soaking tub (Jacuzzi feature options), walk-in shower with dual shower heads, steam unit, aroma therapy system and bench for lounging, warming drawer for toasty towels, private water closet with bidet, direct telephone line, full audio/video access, tanning bed, massage table . . . I could go on and on!

82 UNDEFINED BATH AND CLOSET SPACES

Since no life is spared a challenge or two, is it wrong to wish for only glamorous problems? For instance, in a world where children will go to sleep hungry tonight, I am about to pen a paragraph or two on the relative merits of shared versus individual bathrooms and closets. In the grand scheme of things it is trivial but I've seen some smash-bang-up fights ensue over less trivial concerns, believe you me. If you are blessed with a dacha of such monumental proportions as to warrant this conversation my best recommendation is to fall on your knees, thank your lucky stars (and any godlike entity hovering above your head), and remember how blessed you are. For the rest of us it is negotiation time as we

If you don't live alone, you've likely experienced the ritual of territorial marking. Skirmishes over spatial allocations are most notable in shared bath and closet spaces. The "give" and "take" of international diplomacy should be embraced allowing peace to edge out anarchy in this highly volatile region.

As with most games of strategy, winning the bath and closet game involves having a plan and sticking to it so you can quickly move to a position of advantage. An organizational game plan can put you in the winner's seat. Discover how "yes" and "no" can radically alter your space and storage issues.

divvy up the available space hoping for miracles of epic proportions.

Yes, this truly is the time to make it work—for few are so blessed with space to spare. More often we fantasize about our ideal and make our reality work as best we can. My personal favorite is for a charmingly appointed shared bath with separate closet and dressing areas. In my house, prep time in the bathroom is also catch-up time where "honey-do" lists are updated, calendars confirmed, and the strategies for our daily life are hammered out. But once the game plan is agreed to, my ears cleaned and face shaved, I crave a few moments of blissful silence as I don my daily garb. To each his own in this most personal of places, so whether you are negotiating over existing conditions or designing from scratch, be clear on the concept and stick to your guns. For those with acres of space, draw the lines and claim what's to be yours. For those with greater constraints, greater creativity may be required. Tight urban living may demand you take the cabinet on the right and your partner takes the cabinet on the left, and you rotate bath time based on work schedules. We're not children anymore so talk among yourselves and strike a deal that works.

83 A CLOSET CASE

Since humankind moved out of its first cave, the need to store clothing has dogged our newly shod steps. Initially, it was just a change of animal skins with one or two sandal options. But our closet conundrums have multiplied as our clothing desires expanded with full-on seasonal wardrobes for people who don't have seasons (hugs to all our Los Angeles friends). Closets are big business housing, and you can make a considerable financial investment into them and the clothes you wear, along with spending money on hats, accessories, jewelry, watches, leather goods, luggage, and shoes. The gross domestic product of some city-states falls just shy of what's held behind hermitically sealed doors in the closets of today's movers and shakers. And the key to a closet's overall success is simple—a place for everything and everything in its place. There can be no equivocating, no excuses, no procrastination. I don't care if your closet so small it won't hold the contents of Lady Gaga's "Birkin" bag, neatness counts. Expensive organizational systems and beautifully fitted closet interiors won't save you from yourself.

Follow these three easy steps and win big in the game of small closets. One: edit out things you've not touched in more than nine months. Two: divide and win. Divide your wardrobe by season and, three: high and low. Extra storage can be found high on shelves and beneath beds.

Start by eliminating some of your possessions. If you haven't graced the social pages in that expensive beaded dress or worn those chic but pitifully painful Manolos in more than a year, it's time to give them away. Once you've forced yourself to be brutally honest and removed those important possessions that have hung untouched in your closet for years, you must decide on a reasonable system of organization (by color, by type, by event, and so on). Start rearranging and before you know it, your closet will be organized.

To speed you along the way try these tips for whipping your closet into shape. When it comes to hanging clothes, double rods (one high, one low) are the salvation of many a closet. Double your storage potential and keep all your options right before your eyes. Ladies, for longer garments you know what's needed. Make certain you have clear vertical space to store all your gowns, cloaks, and coats. Most everything else can be covered with our dearly beloved double rods. Shoes, purses, bags, and briefcases all go on the frequency system. Your standard-use items (worn or used on a weekly basis) are to be stored between knee and shoulder height for obvious reasons. Larger items (boots, duffels, and designer handbags of carry-on proportion go knee level and below; smaller items (shoes, handbags, evening clutches, and the occasional hat-in-box) make their way toward the ceiling. Folded shirts and sweaters are best stacked on open shelves (behind glass doors if the budget allows) leaving intimate wear for drawers of which you can never have too many. Ties, belts, and jewelry of all types are best stored in slotted drawers crafted specifically for this purpose. With a lighter load, you'll settle into a slightly simpler gear of life and enjoy the freedom that a bit of organization will bring. And you'll find yourself proclaiming: "Now I can find everything!"

DON'T KNOW ABOUT YOU, but in my bath I want beautiful art and objects a plenty to keep my eyes from lingering on the shocking reality of my naked backside. "My kingdom for distractions!" This bathing beauty looks out over the ocean, all awash in languid light filtered through its sensuous sheers and stately curtains. Sculpture and crystal surround the bubbling basin and all is overlooked by a mirror of antiquity mounted on plate mirror to great effect. Specimen orchids are a living touch, which in this setting are to die for. It's all accomplished in the creamiest of tones, making even the palest of tails pretty again. Who wouldn't enjoy a good soak?

Want more information on the products and resources in this divine bath and closet or to create one of your very own? Try logging onto our website at www.101ThingsIHateAboutYourHouse.com.

11

Home Office

GONE ARE THE DAYS when Dad's office was reserved for either a celebratory brandy and cigar or a closed-door scolding. Most of today's home offices bear little resemblance to that wood-paneled confection of yesteryear. Not that we would mind the spacious layout, the subtle essence of beeswax and tobacco, or the deep, comfortable upholstery; today's version is more akin to command central than to an Oxford idyll. "Wired" and "connected," these tentacles from the workplace have crept into our homes bringing with them waves of wonderfully invasive technology. Assimilating like the Borg, they have melded effortlessly with today's active lifestyle, creating a new breed: the uber home office. It's a force to be dealt with and should be taken for granted only by the foolish—for from these domestic hubs great slices of modern life are monitored, influenced, and controlled.

Whether tucked into a stylish kitchen or allocated to a suite of its own, today's home office adopts a take-no-prisoner approach to managing the lives of its occupants. With technology as a driving force, all manner of monitoring is now possible. As a child, I was convinced that my mother possessed a third eye that could see around corners, look through doors, and hunt down my whereabouts—no matter how stealth my skills of avoidance. Today these fears are well founded (mine just the product of a very effective public relations campaign), for parents everywhere can tap into the powers of technology for that superhuman edge.

84 PRESTIGE FURNITURE

Much like the power suit, the power tie, and the power lunch, the power desk harkens back to the overblown days of the mid-1980s one-upmanship. Status and the vestiges of power seemed easily draped over the arms of the young and upwardly mobile dotting the suburbs and exploding credit card debt. Fast forward and we find motivation has shifted, depositing a greater sense of reality into the search for the perfect desk. Rather than beating the bushes for historically significant monuments from which to command their kingdom, people today seem to place more emphasis on their unique needs allowing provenance to inform their choices rather than dictate. Let's face it, knowing that you have a place for

Slog into your company's corporate headquarters and say thank you for the cubicle, desk, or lap tray they foist on you in exchange for your exemplary services. But work from home and the game changes. You're in charge of selecting the furniture piece you'll rest your elbows on, which will out-dazzle your professional colleagues' space no doubt.

everything and that everything is in its place just might prove more life altering than the pedigreed lineage of the desk your three-year-old decided to mark up with his favorite set of crayons.

On the economy end of the spectrum, please seek a slightly elevated level of design awareness by banishing forever the wood-grained-contact-paper-covering-particle-board offerings touted by the DIY crowd. Better by far to wrap your own plywood creation in faux-python wallpaper and enjoy its uniquely dangerous vibe than endure the embarrassment of the bad college dorm room fare. Even at nineteen, you're just too old for dorm room furniture.

So make a list and check it twice; you're looking for the top five tasks accomplished at your soon-to-be-located desk. Once you understand clearly the tasks at hand, answer the question, "Does this desk help or hinder my success?" If you can't honestly tick off three of the five then your search ain't over so keep on looking. Four out of five should cause you to pause. Five out of five should hear the squeal of plastic as your charge card does its thing.

85 A MAKESHIFT DESK CHAIR

Businesses figured out the benefits of ergonomically correct office furniture years ago, so I shake my head in disbelief when I see homebound executives prop up their sagging bottom lines with folding, breakfast, and dining room chairs. Ergonomics as defined by *Webster* is "an applied science concerned with designing and arranging things people use so that the people and things interact most efficiently and safely." This science should be utilized at home, Dear Hunchbacked Homeowner, so do what's necessary to find and secure a healthy chair to rest your high-powered backside upon. You are more than worth the cost, and the difference in your mood and productivity will be noted by all, because that's what smart design can do.

86 A GROWING PAPER CHASE

Legal or letter size is the core question when we ponder how best to store the acres of dead trees we end up hording both at home and at work. Now that these universes have collided, imagine the storage conundrum faced by planners and power brokers alike. What to keep and what to ditch? Until a more comprehensive response to the dilemma is available (the concept of cloud computing fascinates me), we're stuck filing acres of pulp in drawers of wood and steel. Does anyone but me find this ironic? But, store we must so let's not be complete dolts about it. A measuring tape gets us off to a good start determining exactly how many linear feet of legal (14-inch-long pages) or letter (11-inch-long pages) storage we must conjure up to store our existing collection of documents, receipts, and memoranda.

HOME OFFICE DOS AND DON'TS

Given the space limitations often imposed on today's uber home offices, here are a few storage don'ts on the path to a more gracious home:

DON'T DENY. It's a funny thing about stacks and stacks of vacuous documents from which you can't quite separate yourself: they don't magically disappear. In fact, the single stack quickly becomes two, the twin stacks suddenly become four, and soon you're on your laptop in the garage!

DON'T HIDE. The adjacent closet only holds so much. Better to concede early and pack the banker's boxes before you're branded with the scarlet "H" for hoarder.

DO CONSULT. Make the calls to your legal and tax-type folks about the really important stuff you can't get rid of, but beyond that don't you think it's time for a paper purge and an electronic storage update? Really, how long are you going to hang onto those junior high school lunch menus?

Fabulous file cabinets can be found in steel or wood; just make certain their gliding mechanisms are of the highest quality to ensure the longest wear. Locks on file cabinets are always a good idea and worth the wait if a special order is required. For day-to-day file management, stacking trays or baskets can work well but don't allow them to become holding bins for "to be filed" items or you're right back where you started, and that's not beautiful.

 ## PISS-POOR LIGHTING

Under the best conditions, there's little exciting about work; it is what it is, a necessary evil moving us toward a goal. That this ubiquitous truth has invaded our home territory might just rub us the wrong way, but it does little to diminish our need to produce exceptional results. And it doesn't take a brain surgeon to know that those results don't happen in the dark.

As dearly as I love candlelight for all things social, when it's time to get down to business you're either an Ebenezer Scrooge or just plain silly if you think you'll conquer the high and mighty worlds of commerce while chipping away at projects by the light of a single, shrinking candlestick. You score points for the romantic gesture but at the same time earn a big fat bitch slap for your less than functional antics. Put a light where a light wants to be and anywhere there's a work surface qualifies for such sight-specific illumination. Within the confines of the home office this typically means:

- At least one desk lamp (by now all your lamps have dimmers, right?) with a maximum 100-watt bulb. I prefer the bulbs to be pale pink or for the lamp shade to have a pale silk lining.

- A reading lamp next to your favorite chair.
- A hanging or ceiling fixture, of some description, offering general illumination.

As is the case with any room, pockmarked ceilings filled with recessed can lights should be ignored for daily use. The occasional solar blast from these developer-driven distractions should be reserved for use by your cleaning lady or the random hunt necessitated by the separation of either a contact lens from a guest's eye or a diamond from a ring or brooch.

Daily use of such blinding light is just unflattering. In stressful times, the possibility of chucking random objects in their general direction becomes a real threat, which reminds me of the timeless showering of sparks—when Suzanne Sugarbaker's baton tangled with a transformer high above in the Miss Georgia competition—and the night the lights went out in Georgia!

88 EXTRANEOUS TECHNOLOGY

With space at a minimum in most home offices, the accumulation of anything that might be considered surplus is best avoided before your precious home office resembles a storage locker on the Island of Misfit Office Equipment. Personal discipline will distinguish your office from that of your BFF's when you successfully edit from your line of sight all unnecessary electronic gadgets. The tendency to collect, then store purchases that, at the time, seemed reasonable all too quickly becomes unreasonable. Edit, edit, and edit again.

While it may be true that the only difference between men and boys is the cost of their toys, the advent of touchy technology makes us hard-pressed to single out one gender over the other when it comes to techno-hoarding. For a great swath of both sexes, the existence of an item with an on/off switch, an LED screen, and a power source serves as reasons enough to get one as soon as possible. This, as an isolated idea, is hardly the end of gracious living. What does threaten to burst the seams of an otherwise beautifully orchestrated home office is what I refer to as the "Santa effect." The Santa effect occurs when we long to own some new toy or technical treat only to buy it, open the box, lose some degree of interest, and set down the slightly less interesting item on top of the growing pile of the-thrill-is-gone toys. My how things don't change. Simple rule to live by with pos-sessions of a technical or aesthetic bent: if your hands have not gripped it, flipped it, or put it to work in the most recent three months, chances are there is no real need to pretend it's impor-tant to your life. Sell it, donate it, or in someway or another get its carcass out of your house. You will enjoy the diminished clutter and will never miss whatever was lurking at the bottom of the pile.

89 WHEN EXPECTATIONS CAN'T FIND A SEAT

Not that I'm the controlling type, but I just chuckle when friends or clients complain that they never get any work done. They insist on filling their beautifully executed home office with sofas, settees, lounge, and club chairs that populate this haven of productivity. Shocking that nothing gets done. Home offices are for work, and unless your work involves a cast of thousands, at very close prox-imity, install exactly the number of seats required and not one more. Depending on staffing demands, I advocate a primary seat for *your* primary seat, a work chair for the occasional assistant or colleague (not too comfortable for obvious reasons), and a com-fortable reading chair with ottoman to which you may retire when your state of affairs are better faced with your feet up. Use less if you require less, but not one seat more than you intend to have filled. And when they are filled, they will by partners, friends, and the neighbor's kids; and you'll never get your precious work done.

 NOWHERE TO STICK IT

Oh, the wisdom to be discovered in the games of children. Go ahead, put on a blindfold, spin in place, and then stumble across a crowded room as you attempt to pinpoint a particularly specific spot. Sounds like just another day at the office for some. For the mere mortals out there struggling to recall every little detail of every little transaction that crosses your path, you are not alone. And there is hope. The answer is in the simple pinboard. Many years ago it occurred to me that this fixture, which exists in most design business offices, might be a boon for those working at home, trying to juggle work, family, friends, and hordes of complete strangers each vying for those three lingering brain

cells. Whether purchased from an online catalog or whipped up by a local workroom, a stylish pinboard, giant in size (ideally 48-inches wide and more than 72-inches tall), and decorated to fit your stylistic fancy (fabric covered, zigzagged with trim, gimp, or leather strips, and outfitted with coordinating pushpins or thumbtacks), can become a secret weapon in navigating your way through the minefield of daily life.

Alarm systems, advanced locking devices and large, scary dogs do much to keep intruders out of our homes. This is a good thing. But what can be done to assist an absentminded homemaker regarding the location of life's important documents? Creating one central location for all-important documents, then safeguarding them from prying eyes and distracted minds will give any homeowner a sense of security.

91 NOT FEELING SAFE

Like children in their Easter best on the West Lawn of the White House, the scramble and search that ensues in homes everywhere when an important document is needed can be quite comical if you are merely an observer—comical, unless it is you who can't find your passport, auto title, or birth certificate. Amazing how quickly the humor fades. So what's a stylish homeowner to do? Often, I'm laughed at when I deliver the simple answer, though for

many a homeowner the obvious never crosses their minds. The straightforward and stylish answer to storing important documents is a safe. The size and complexity of the unit will vary depending on your needs.

If the family jewels, antique gun collection, and every stock and bond certificate you've ever owned need storage, there are walk-in vaults available that will do just fine. Not so dripping with jewels or precious collectibles and just need a place to house the family's birth certificates and passports? Then a small (16 x 10 x 24-inch) unit is better suited to your needs. And there's everything in between. So be a smart shopper and know what you're storing before you start shopping.

Regardless, the office is a sensible location for a safe's installation. Never divulge its specific placement to the outside world. When bolted to the floor, wall, or cabinetry even the smallest unit can offer a repository for valuables of all types. Remember a gracious home is a thoughtful home and that starts with thoughtfully managing the things most important to you.

92 WHEN FAMILIARITY BREEDS CONTEMPT

Whether working from home full time or one day per week, the impetus to strive for maximum levels of success remains. Every advantage must be leveraged, every tool utilized, and every course charted that will lead us to the heights of glory and the rewards of wisdom, fame, and fortune. To me, it just doesn't add up to think you will be climbing these heights in a worn-out pair of sweatpants and a holey T-shirt.

Having worked from home and from a traditional office, my thoughts on the issue of dressing for work at home are fueled by firsthand sartorial research. Never one to beat around the bush, I believe working from home does not license one to become a first-rate, if closeted, slob. We experience a mental pick-me-up when we dress for success no matter how casual the path to success may be. Admittedly, a bespoke suit and its custom accoutrements provide a soaring case of overkill for a day of home-based productivity; but

with similar, if slightly, opposing logic so, too, would it be to don worn-out sweatpants, a favorite, if threadbare, T-shirt, and rancid gym socks. When one works from the house, appropriateness reigns supreme, whether one day a week or for the rest of your life. Honor the importance of the work you do by dressing the part each and every day.

93 Doors That Don't Lock

In a perfect world, well, everything would be perfect. Lions would recline with lambs, we would always have good parking, and a bad hair day would be a thing of mythic lore. As of this writing, such rarified existences only materialize in celluloid fantasies leaving us to deal with the nuts and bolts, the broken nails, and shockingly bad hair. A collective "ugh" can be heard. With reality wrapping its ridiculous tentacles through and around the fabric of our lives, there are few options left but to lock the door, pop in our ear buds, and crank up the tunes until the madness marches by. Key to this plan of action is the ability to lock the door of your office. If you are blessed with a space of your own then the retrofit is a quick fix and you're ready to shun the world at the drop of a newscaster's cue card. If your home office does double duty, sharing its arsenal of professional equipment with other household objectives, then a bit of sensitivity might be required. A case for personal privacy, not to mention security, can be made for a locking mechanism on the door of most every room in the house. Don't become the executive who cries wolf; wisely applied, a locked door can buy you sanity when all the world is going to hell in a smartly lined handbasket.

No home is such an egalitarian oasis as not to require locks on doors. The smallest of children might require safety mechanisms to avoid a scary and unintended lock-in, but beyond this youthful accommodation, locks provide an exclamation point to an otherwise politely closed door. Children and adults should take note.

Here's another corner of my Los Angeles home, my office away from the office. Because space was at a premium this room doubles as a media center; behind the bypass screens on the right of the picture is a projection television and all the other media necessities for audio and video. But, at the heart of it all, this is where I work when I'm home. My favorite desk by Jansen, comfortable seating, diffused lighting, and the sectional covered in super-heavy-duty linen velvet. In this room I've had great productive afternoons and wonderfully entertaining movie nights all effortlessly handled by opening and closing a wall of rolling panels. The graphic punch of the Chinese calligraphy screen puts a finishing touch on a favorite space.

Curious to learn more about the products and resources in my home office or want to create one of your very own? Try logging onto our website at www.101ThingsIHateAboutYourHouse.com.

12

Mudroom

Like a Pig In . . .

THE TRANSITION FROM GUEST to adopted family member is often heralded by instructions to bypass the main entrance in favor of the family entrance, known to many as the mudroom. Like a shot of adrenaline administered directly to the heart, access to a home through this familial portal propels you into the core of domestic life. No matter how grand the domicile's façade, you can count on enough piles of mud-caked boots, weather-dampened jackets, and brutalized sporting equipment to level life's playing field. Nothing like the detritus of real life to remind us of our mud-based humanity. Having clawed our way up from a complexion nourishing swamp, it seems fitting to wrap up our tour on gracious living in a room dedicated to the mud in our life.

94 HIGH-MAINTENANCE FLOORING CHOICES

The elements conspire with a vengeance to do unspeakable damage on as much of the world as possible. We shelter ourselves, in houses of wood, stone, and glass, hoping to avoid the element's relentless affronts; but at some point what is outside must come in. This is when the room of mud, whether a devoted space or a corner kept for just such a time, shines. Water, in all its blustery forms, fails to wrinkle a well-tended brow when soggy feet are firmly planted on stony (or other impenetrable material) ground. When shopping for material in this category, look at all manner of natural stone (granite, limestone, marble, slate) in a honed or natural finish. Anything polished will be too slick for this high-traffic area. Silly, bordering on the ridiculous, is a high-maintenance floor installed in what is arguably the Grand Central Station of your home. Better to just fling wide the door to the wailings and beatings of Mamma Nature than to invite the conceit of

a delicate flooring material in this, the buffer zone. For what is a room of mud if it's not a stalwart defender of the home's inner sanctums from the onslaught of the world at large? Standing toe to toe with the best of your impervious floor would be the furnishings, fixtures, and built-ins that complete the ensemble cast. Not a place for the delicate or demure, this is the place to cast the best of the rough-and-tumble crowd, allowing them to whip some heavy-duty ass along the way.

95 PILES OF SHOES

At the height of excavation, Boston's Big Dig looked suspiciously similar to some mudrooms I've seen, where piles of shoes and boots have reached epic proportion. Some people, I fear, reach a state of disillusionment with their condition and convince themselves that "purchasing new" might be the only solution. This does nothing for the festering pile of wet and worn tennis, track, football, soccer, jogging, dancing, biking, climbing, walking, hiking, and racing shoes stacked in their mudroom. Mix in a healthy dose of boots (all types and sizes), and you have a strategic organizational challenge to furrow the brows of MacArthur's best. Cubbies and cabinets seem the best line of defense against the cumulative forces of the dark podiatric arts and are most successful after a major pick or purge offensive. Dear Mavens of the Mud, the drill is simple but effective. Plunge a well-protected hand into the pile of misfit shoes, raising high the results of your efforts. Turn to the owner and they either take the shoe (then rummage for its partner) or agree to purge the pair, much to the joy of your local charity. With the pile reduced to selected stacks of the dearly beloveds, it's time to assign them a new home. Wee-little labels on cabinets and cubbies are static reminders for minds that wander. It's entirely possible that a reminder or six might be necessary to jog the minds of those you love without the use of labels, but then what are those running shoes for anyway?

In the buffer zone of our mudroom, a clearly established storage place for inclement grade shoes is a first order of business. Training household members to utilize their cubbies or cabinets might be the more difficult task. Training new dogs to handle this old task, at times, can be as difficult as dealing with the older of the breed. A night in the garage usually gets the attention of both young and old!

96   COATS AND HATS EVERYWHERE

As a child did you ever play hide-and-seek in the house? If you did, you might have enjoyed the sensorial thrill of hiding in the back of a coat closet. There's something heady about its mélange of color, texture, and aroma; the mix of wools, furs, and leathers, and the lingering ghosts of cologne and perfume. They all conspire to construct cellular memories held firm to this day. Unfortunately, the room of mud doesn't share these claustro-fabulous features. Here, we see damp coats and cloaks randomly tossed at, not necessarily on hooks weighted down with multiple garments and their weather-born residue. We can hope to avoid catching a whiff of stale, moldy air as we wrestle with the piles and corral these seasonal garments into some semblance of dry order.

When couched in the context of protecting valuable assets, the proper daily care for the clothes on our backs becomes an issue of considerable importance. These wonderful warm and stylish numbers aren't free, and shame on the soul who doesn't raise their maintenance a peg or two

In the current economic climate, only a fool would suggest wasting money. If I'm not mistaken, the slovenly care of an existing asset would qualify as foolish behavior. Particularly when it relates to thousands of dollars invested in seasonally smart clothing. Waste not, want not—to borrow a dusty old phrase.

above that found in a dorm room or frat house. If cubbies are your method of controlling the madness, be realistic about the relationship between allocated space and hooks, as this will inform your minions of their hanging options. Three hooks spaced about six inches apart for each cubbie is usually about right, with your cubbies at a comfortable 20-inches wide should give everyone on your team space enough to do the right thing.

The hunt for perfection in the home of your dreams, will keep you awake for years to come. Don't reinvent the wheel when it's not necessary. Check out an array of cubby designs that will save you time and money at www.101 ThingsIHateAbout YourHouse.com.

97 A MOUND OF BAGS

In our mad dash through the calisthenics of daily life, all of us, male or female, young or old avail ourselves of the ease offered by bagging it. Whether we're toting around eco-friendly grocery bags with bold, zippy graphics, tossing our iPad into a sleek leather briefcase, schlepping around a costume change, toting personal hair and makeup supplies, carrying a teacup Rottweiler in a "Birkin" bag the size of a shipping crate, or dragging about a bulging knapsack filled with fuel for our scholarly pursuits, we all rely on a bag or two to get us through the day.

Where, Dear Bag-Digging Darlings, do the containers of our lives live when not weighted down by our lotions, potions, gadgets, and gizmos? Typically they reside just inside the door through which we enter the house. It's a little-known law of Murphy that states that the distance a bag is carried into a home is directly proportional to the perishable nature of its contents. Dairy products and raw meat seem to propel bags all the way into the kitchen, while your everyday briefcase, purse, or backpack falls within inches of the mudroom door. Good design can work many miracles, but altering this specific DNA coding is a push for even the most seasoned professional. I recommend multiple table surfaces, a personalized cubby or cabinet with shelves and hooks (for the anal retentive among us), and the threat of forfeiture should our bag-o-the-day end up loitering on the floor in the hall of mud.

98 A LOAD OF LUGGAGE

As an inveterate traveler, I know the value of good luggage as well as the effort and energy required to keep it in tip-top shape. The scuffs, scrapes, and gouges borne by your favorite, faithful roll-on bag provide the telling signs of your careless travel preparation or worse yet, your lackluster storage system.

With all vestiges of travel glamour having evaporated like Kanye West's dignity at the MTV Video Music Awards, we must

cling to any and all aspirations that might distinguish us from the other peasants groveling their way through security's less-than-venial maze. Dazzling luggage, pristine and fresh (even if not the most expensive), might set us apart just enough to wrangle from the underpaid, overworked counter jockey the one last upgrade to middle-class still available. Stranger things have happened. But you're dead in the waters of common-class travel if your luggage looks like an aging actor on a midnight joyride through Malibu. I find the luxury of storage and servicing my luggage in a cabinet or closet of an appropriate size in the mudroom to be a little bit of traveler's heaven. I have space to store my travel set in one location—no more scavenger hunts through closets both near and far. I keep a small maintenance and repair kit with the stored luggage that keeps me looking my best as I march my way through modern-day purgatory otherwise known as the nation's airports. But, dammit, doesn't my luggage look great?

99 ERRANT SPORTS EQUIPMENT

What would the perfectly gracious home be without a few hiccups and hurdles along the way? Far be it for me to besmirch the athletes of the world. As with all stereotypes, they exist for a reason. Usually, a very good reason. I've been known to show up and cheer, like a schoolgirl, for a sports team populated by the young children of my friends and neighbors. Sports build character, promote healthy living, encourage teamwork, nurture sportsmanlike competition, and thus get my enthusiastic "rah-rah" every single time.

My celebrating comes to a screeching halt when those little field jockeys tumble into the house depositing flatbeds of gear on every horizontal surface in sight. Okay, I understand youthful enthusiasm (in the case

The novel concept that "things only work if you do" is best writ in blazing neon letters so the youngsters of the house can't miss its pointed message. Storage cubbies, closets, and the like can be artfully designed, meticulously crafted, and installed with the grace of a ballerina. If their purpose is ignored, whether by omission or commission, then what's the use? Why bother?

of a win) and adolescent depression on the days we lose, but I
see no excuse for these piles to
linger while there's still breath in
the lungs of those young, healthy
sportsmen and women. Whatever
form it takes, the perfectly appointed room of mud supports ath-
letics at every turn, most graciously
through ample and well-ventilated
storage space. Install, when you're able,
slot-fronted cabinets, lockers, or chests into
which these piles of equipment may be poured. If
closets exist co-opt them and install the appropriate stacking, hanging, and storing systems for the sports represented by
your band of merry athletes. Then drill into their adroit little heads
the necessity of caring for their gear lest it disappear for good.

The mudroom's ability to provide effective storage for the sports enthu-siast teeters on three keys principles: storage, ventilation, and cleaning. Can your room for mud adequately store all necessary equipment? Does your storage offer adequate ventilation? And, finally, is there ample space for the equipment to be taken out and properly cleaned from time to time?

100 WHEN PET CARE IS IGNORED

Anyone with a pet understands full well who rules the house.
Be they little or big, canine or feline, pets manage to weave their
wonder through every aspect of life—as it should be if you ask me.

Just plain silly are homes where cat and dogs are restricted to the laundry room, kitchen, or mudroom. Excuses fly and fall on dead ears. If behavior issues cause the banishment, bring in help to resolve the issues. Pet shrinks and trainers that are more traditional abound with many who actually know what they're doing. So

don't be shy about fully integrating your animals into the life of your house. If you have the luxury of a mudroom, you certainly should have a cabinet or two to consolidate Fifi or Fido's collection of favorite (and necessary) things. As with your luggage, the act of consolidating pet paraphernalia streamlines your life, eliminating senseless hunts for comb, brush, or medicated shampoos. If you've gone over the top with your room of mud and have space to spare, who wouldn't covet a doggie bathing station? While sounding like a ridiculous extravagance to anyone who hasn't tried to bathe a standard poodle in the guest room's bathtub, the pet-bathing station (for a pet owner who doesn't export the care and cleaning of their precious four-legged friend) could be the deal of the decade. The water-friendly realm of your room for mud provides a convenient location.

Pets, like children, require toys, gismos, and gadgets to keep them entertained, primped, and pretty. So make sure to allocate cabinet space specifically for the pets in your life.

101 SCATTERED CLUTTER FILLING DRAWERS AND CLOSETS

While cordoning off space, give a thought to other task-oriented household chores that might benefit from an additional cubby,

The supplies, tools, and accoutre-ments that stock a successful mud-room attest to the room's far-reaching impact on daily life in any home. Like a medical crash kit, ready for every emergency, these cabinets and cases become a repository for every house-hold trick and tool known to man. When a need presents itself you know just where to go, no questions asked.

cabinet, or closet and that other-wise might be scattered through-out the house. If the decorating gods have been good to you and you've got space to spare, carve out just one little slice of space as an overflow zone for ironing the family laundry. Even if it's just a bit of floor space on which to set up your tools for ironing, the bonanza of an alternate work space can breathe life into an otherwise dreary house-hold chore. Hate the thought of pressing shirts, socks, and linens in the darkness of your basement? Commandeer a corner of your mudroom near a beautiful bank of windows and let the sunshine in. Surely, the board for ironing and a few sup-plies can be squeezed into a nearby closet. Find a shelf for the iron-ing basket, lavender water, and spray starch, and you're set with a change of scenery.

As a hub of activity, the mudroom can rival the kitchen and thus should be prepared for a long list of the inevitable and invariable. Consider all the minor tools and supplies needed to run a house of any size. House hammers, screwdrivers, pliers, wire snips, picture hangers, electrical tape, duct tape, and museum wax should be placed in a basic tool box and always at the ready. Stock lightbulbs, dimmer switches, and extra trim pieces for your recessed light fixtures (necessary evil that they are) all gathered in one place, which can make home projects a snap when they come up.

SNUGGLED AMONG THE TREES AND PERCHED ON A BLUFF overlooking the ocean, this delightful mudroom provides a stylish and practical introduction to this jewel of a home. While not a huge room, its fitted cabinets of cherry and maple make a strong architectural statement while comfortably housing the outdoor gear of a young and active family. Slate on the floor gives Mom one less thing to worry about; and between the cubbies, cabinets, and baskets there's something warm for every head in the house. I'm intrigued by the abundance of natural light that makes this secondary room feel very important. The clients view it as an important room where they enter the house and are encouraged to shed all the unnecessary elements of the world outside (yes, I've heard laptops and mobile phones mentioned) and enjoy time with the family. Now that's beautiful.

Conclusion

WE'VE RUN OUT OF HOUSE but not of things to ponder, take note of, or to take action on. Every house is a growing, evolving entity that asks for attention, care, and consistent nourishment. Your home provides a rich tapestry of opportunities, experiences, and memories in the making. When our purpose is to elevate our living experience from the ordinary to the exceptional, when we've taken steps to educate ourselves away from the faux pas and toward the fabulous, then we are well on our way to a more beautiful, gracious way of life. So go, enjoy the place you call home. Have fun making it a more beautiful place to live; when your friends ask what has changed, you can smile and tell them the truth: you have fallen in love with your home, again. Now that's beautiful.

Every house is a growing, evolving entity.

Acknowledgments

JAMES SWAN WOULD LIKE TO THANK: If home is where the heart is, then my emotional center is dotted across the country, thanks to my collection of friends and relations. On the West Coast, thank you to Wes Wheadon, who never stopped believing and still spins the best music I've ever tapped a toe to. To Steve Tyler for laughing at my work and helping me believe I might have something humorous to say. To Damien Ramos, the best EA in the world, who has never been at a loss for a smile and an optimistic word. To Sherry Knack, my high-school English teacher, who taught me to love the written word. Maybe one day I'll get the hang of jotting them down? To Wade Davis, for the safest place I've ever known. To my parents John and Joan, sisters Judy and Joyce and my niece Katie: you may not always have understood, but you've always loved me and as Grandpa once told me, "Love is all that really matters." Shifting to the East Coast: where would I be without Jeffrey Kahan, the best of best friends? Cynthia Finnemore Simonds: I would not have survived these past months without your hugs. To Tyler Reed, who recently slipped into my heart and who is welcome to stay for a very long time: yes, it is true what they say about penguins. To the memory of Max and Mickey, my Yorkshire Terriers so lovingly memorialized in Stan's illustrations: I miss you every day. To Stan and Carol, without whom this book would never have happened: this adventure feels like a great big beginning. I can't imagine sharing all that is ahead with anyone else but you.

CAROL BEGGY WOULD LIKE TO THANK: My family and friends, who rallied around me during this process like they were called to an Amish barn raising. I didn't need the events of the last year to know I had your support, but how wonderful it was to be buoyed by you each and every day. To my sister Pat for all of it, but mostly for never using that medical power of attorney. My sister Terry for picking up the mantle of family reporter and for keeping this family functioning. To both of my sisters for "girling up" my house so that Jim would hate nothing. My brother, Mickey, for being there when he was needed and using his considerable talents to make my house a home. My sister-in-law, Margie, for always reworking some schedule to make it all come together. To the next Beggy generation, Matthew James, Martina Michela, and Michael Daniel, know that you can be whatever you dream. Mom, I'll just apologize for being a tough nut, but hey, I'm the baby, gotta love me. Right? To Bill Brett for your unerring advice and unwavering friendship. To Jan Saragoni for letting me be part of the "& Company" and opening new doors. Chris Haynes, you're the closest thing I have to a baby brother, so watch out. Michela, Ed, Jayne, and the rest of the Larsons, thank you for always finding an extra seat at the table. To Susan and Bruce for twenty years of having my back and giving me my own home. To Denise Pons Leone for supporting her friends the way audiences have always cheered for her. To the Donstons: Colm, Brogan, and Trinity, thank you for letting me be part of your universe. To the entire staff of Massachusetts General Hospital for getting me back to "normal." To the late Butchie Doe and Handy for being the best beings to share a home with. And to Jim and Stan, a big mushy hug for picking me on their dodgeball team.

STANLEY A. MEYER, WOULD LIKE TO THANK: My partner, Arnis, who over the course of a year and a half watched as thousands of pieces of research, idea sketches, and renderings were put up on the wall and then taken down again . . . in no specific order. Barney Bainbridge, our cat who posed for endless hours as I tried to capture "the moment," but not necessarily enjoying the poses Arnis had to hold him in. Nicole Page and Heidi Reavis for their continued love, support, and figuring out the legality of my new title as "Illustrator." My rendering and color mentors (as well as dear friends) Jose "Hochi" Asiatico and Bill Bilke, who at the last minute giggled and laughed with me as we slaved for hours upon end pulling the renderings into one world as we enjoyed a cocktail or two. My dear family and friends who, supporting my need to stay committed to the work, would come to visit from time to time to see how the wall of sketches was changing and evolving. "Mother" Herb Camburn, for telling me I was talented and would always have a job as a designer in the theater. And lastly my mother Marion, who in her own right was a brilliant artist, though she never had the opportunity to really explore her creativity but lived out her art fantasy through my work and career as an artist in the theater. Thanks for the collections of the heart, Mom and Dad! I miss you dearly.

THE "101 THINGS" CREATIVE TEAM would like to thank Janice Pieroni and Story Arts Management for getting us here. What a journey and we could not have done this without you. Carol De Tine, AIA and Carriage House Studio, for a most beautiful mudroom attached to a most charming house. A round of thanks to our photographers Tim Street Porter, Erhard Pfeiffer, Sam Gray, and Paula Roberts. Our editor, Michele Matrisciani, and the HCI team, we are humbled by how easily and readily you embraced our project and took a risk in branching out into the world of home design. To those who have joined our online communities and given us feedback and support, we have only things we love about what you have shared with us. And to Erach Screwvala, our New York legal eagle, for finding a way for us to exist and embark on this journey.

Index of Illustrations

Index

About the Authors

JAMES SWAN is head of New Wall Enterprises, a Beverly Hills-based design and lifestyle group focused on delivering smart design daily to consumers across the country and around the world. As a lifestyle leader he has been featured in *House & Garden* magazine, *House Beautiful,* and the *Los Angeles Times.* He wrote a "Trends & Shopping" column for *House & Garden* magazine, and continues the dialogue on his own design blog, The Design Quotient (www.designquotient.com). Adding author (as a contributor to Curbed.com and other sites) and speaker (NeoCon West) to his accomplishments has further broadened his influence. A Facebook page features many of the principles discussed in *101 Things I Hate About Your House* with inspired interaction from a growing following of fans of Swan's work.

Swan's career took off back in Northern California at a noted San Francisco architecture firm where he managed residential interiors. After that, Los Angeles beckoned; specifically, the prestigious firm of Frank K. Pennino & Associates, where as senior designer he managed high-profile projects and earned a reputation for refined classical design that succinctly reflected his clients' lives. In 1999, Swan opened his own firm in Beverly Hills. His talents earned him Vox Vodka/*Out* Magazine's Designer of the Year Award. In 2009 Ballard Designs (www.ballarddesigns.com) announced their collaboration with Swan, their first with a nationally known designer. His collection of home furnishings and accessories will debut in 2011.

From 2005 to 2009, Swan was a member of the executive board of directors of the Gay and Lesbian Victory Fund. His other community commitments include PAWS/LA, which assists with the care of pets for people living with disabilities, and KidSmart, an art education foundation for inner-city youth. In his free time, Swan may be found indulging his passion for gardening, skiing, and travel. He divides his time between Beverly Hills, Boston, and Pemaquid, Maine.

CAROL BEGGY is an award-winning writer and editor who has worked at several eastern Massachusetts publications, including *The Boston Globe,* where she worked for more than ten years. While at the *Globe,* Beggy was the founding editor of the *Globe*'s West section, was a co-author of the "Names" column, and wrote the popular column "On Location," which appeared on the cover of the *Globe*'s Sunday Real Estate section. Previous to her return to the *Globe,* Beggy was an editor of the *MetroWest Daily News* in Framingham where she directed the features and lifestyle coverage.

Beggy keeps her writing chops fresh through her work for several national publications, including Niche Media and its regional glossy *Boston Common* magazine; a monthly column for the *Boston Irish Reporter*; and the bimonthly backpage feature for *Stuff* magazine. Her work has also appeared in *Boston* magazine, *The Irish Times, ARTnews, Los Angeles Times, Chicago Tribune, People* magazine, *Us* magazine, and numerous other publications. She also worked as a freelance producer for CBS News.

A cum laude graduate of Northeastern University, Beggy has studied at Harvard University's Extension School. She is a Pittsburgh native and has the honor and horror of being a fan of the Pittsburgh Steelers, Pittsburgh Penguins, and the Pittsburgh Pirates.

Among her many collaborations are three books with renowned photographer Bill Brett: *Boston, All One Family* (foreword by Robert B. Parker); *Boston, An Extended Family* (foreword by Doris Kearns Goodwin); and *Boston, A Year in the Life* (foreword by David G. Mugar). The three books were all published by Commonwealth Editions. The duo is being joined by Brett's daughter, Kerry Brett, for a fourth project, *Boston Inspirational Women*, which is scheduled to be published by Applewood Books in 2011. Beggy also was part of *The Boston Globe* team that produced *Ted Kennedy: Scenes from an Epic Life*, published by Simon & Schuster in March, 2009.

Beggy is the founder and principal partner of Raw Bar Productions, which consults on film, radio, and television projects. She is a marketing and public relations consultant to Rustic Kitchen and its *The Cooking Show*. Beggy is a senior consultant for Saragoni & Company and frequently collaborates with the Balboni Communications Group. She was writer and story producer for the 2009 launch of *styleboston*, a 30-minute lifestyle TV show that airs weekly in New England.

Beggy is a member of the Authors Guild and the Women in Film and Video/New England. A recipient of the Urban League of Eastern Massachusetts President's Award, she is a member of the Civic Participation committee in The Alliance for Digital Equality's review of the city of Boston.

Illustrator STANLEY A. MEYER has more than four dozen credits as a scenic designer/production designer that have earned him numerous awards and nominations, including an American Theatre Wing Design Award nomination; a New York Outer Critics Circle Award nomination; a National Broadway Theatre Award nomination; a Los Angeles Ovation Award Nomination; THEA Award winner—Best Outdoor Nighttime Spectacular for *Peter Pan's Neverland* at Universal Studios Japan; IAPPA Brass Ring Award winner—Best Outdoor Daytime Spectacular for SeaWorld's *Blue Horizons*, a stadium show that features a cast of dolphins, whales, birds, trainers, acrobats, and divers which can be seen both in Orlando and San Diego; and numerous Los Angeles Drama Logue Awards for his work at the Grove Shakespeare Festival in Southern California.

His critically acclaimed work includes the smash-hit show *Disney's Beauty and the Beast* (the sixth longest running show in Broadway history) and the world premiere of Elton John and Tim Rice's *Aida* (Alliance Theatre, Atlanta). Meyer also was the first recipient of The League of American Theatres and Producers, National Broadway Award for his design of the North America Tour of *Disney's Beauty and the Beast.*

Recent credits include *Barnum's Funundrum,* the 140th edition of the Ringling Brothers Barnum & Bailey Circus; Alice Cooper's 2007 Tour and Cooper's 2009 and 2010 *Theatre of Death* Tour; the 2010 national tour of

Disney's Beauty and the Beast; architectural redesign for SeaWorld Orlando's iconographic sky tower; The Steve Miller Band 2010 *Bingo!* Tour; *One Ocean* —the new Shamu show opening 2011 at all three of SeaWorld's venues; and Tim Burton's *Alice in Wonderland*, the Broadway musical.

Meyer's work includes conceptual design and development for Nike, Sony, PGAV, Bounce Events, Inmotion Entertainment, Thinkwell Design & Production, Busch Gardens in Williamsburg and Tampa, Madame Tussaud's Las Vegas, Universal Studios Orlando, Clear Channel Family Entertainment's national tour of *Time for Teletubbies!*, design segment for IKEA's TV show, *Space for Living,* a plethora of Disney industrials, parades, and special events including *Mickey's Nutcracker,* filmed for The Disney Channel, Cyndi Lauper's *True Colors* tour featuring the B-52s, the Clicks, and Colton Ford, *The New Nutcracker Ballet* for The Lone Star Ballet, Texas, and *Disney Live! Three Classic Fairy Tales,* Feld Entertainment Inc.

A native of Hemet, a rural farm town in Southern California, Meyer graduated from Mount San Jacinto College and California State University Long Beach before being accepted at the Mason Gross School of Arts at Rutgers University, where he received a Master's of Fine Arts in theatrical design. He is an active supporter of the Transgender Legal Defense & Education Fund. Meyer lives in New York City with his partner Arnis Robeznieks, a pastry chef. They have a cat named Barney Bainbridge, who adopted them at an ASPCA shelter. To view more of Stanley's design please visit www.stanleyameyerdesign.com.

What I Hate About My Entry Way

What to Do About My Entry Way

_____

_____

_____

_____

_____

_____

_____

_____

_____

_____

_____

_____

_____

_____

What I Hate About My Powder Room

What to Do About My Powder Room

_____

_____

_____

_____

_____

_____

_____

_____

_____

_____

_____

_____

_____

_____

What I Hate About My Living Room

What to Do About My Living Room

_____

_____

_____

_____

_____

_____

_____

_____

_____

_____

_____

_____

_____

_____

What I Hate About My Dining Room

What to Do About My Dining Room

_____

_____

_____

_____

_____

_____

_____

_____

_____

_____

_____

_____

_____

_____

What I Hate About My Kitchen

What to Do About My Kitchen

_____

_____

_____

_____

_____

_____

_____

_____

_____

_____

_____

_____

What I Hate About My Family Room

What to Do About My Family Room

_____

_____

_____

_____

_____

_____

_____

_____

_____

_____

_____

_____

_____

_____